Exam 70-413:
Designing and Implementing a Server Infrastructure

Exam Ref

Steve Suehring

Published with the authorization of Microsoft Corporation by:

O'Reilly Media, Inc.
1005 Gravenstein Highway North
Sebastopol, California 95472

ISBN: 978-0-7356-7367-0

1 2 3 4 5 6 7 8 9   QG   7 6 5 4 3 2

Printed and bound in the United States of America.

Microsoft Press books are available through booksellers and distributors worldwide. If you need support related to this book, email Microsoft Press Book Support at *mspinput@microsoft.com*. Please tell us what you think of this book at *http://www.microsoft.com/learning/booksurvey*.

Acquisitions and Developmental Editor: Ken Jones
Production Editor: Holly Bauer
Editorial Production: Box Twelve Communications
Technical Reviewer: Brian Svidergol
Copyeditor: Susan Shaw Dunn
Indexer: Ginny Munroe
Cover Design: Twist Creative • Seattle
Cover Composition: Zyg Group, LLC
Illustrator: Rebecca Demarest

To Rebecca.

Contents at a Glance

Contents

What do you think of this book? We want to hear from you!

Microsoft is interested in hearing your feedback so we can continually improve our
books and learning resources for you. To participate in a brief online survey, please visit:

www.microsoft.com/learning/booksurvey/

Introduction

This *Exam Ref* is designed to assist you with studying for the MCITP exam 70-413, "Designing and Implementing a Server Infrastructure." This exam focuses on both the use of server technologies to solve particular design objectives as well as the implementation of those designs to meet certain objectives. The exam has network-related objectives and calls on your experience with Windows Server and related technologies such as DirectAccess, VPNs, DNS, and DHCP.

The 70-413 exam is meant for large, enterprise-scale organizations and their needs. Passing the exam demonstrates your knowledge and experience with enterprise server technologies.

This book will review every concept described in the following exam objective domains:

- Plan and deploy a server infrastructure
- Design and implement network infrastructure services
- Design and implement network access services
- Design and implement an Active Directory infrastructure (logical)
- Design and implement an Active Directory infrastructure (physical)

Even though this book covers all the technologies involved in each exam objective, it's not meant to be a brain dump of questions that you'll see on the exam. In fact, this book is meant to be used as a supplement to your own experience with and a study of the relevant technologies in each objective. As you read the book, if you come across areas that you are less familiar with, you should follow up on that area to obtain additional knowledge. In many cases, the book provides links to the relevant areas in TechNet, but you should also pursue this area using every available tool at your disposal, including other areas of Microsoft's website, forums, and first-hand experience. In fact, you should deploy your own infrastructure for this exam to match the recommended lab scenarios covered not only in this book but also in the documentation from Microsoft on these subject areas. Microsoft offers trial versions of all software involved in this exam, and you can create a virtualized infrastructure to help your study of the exam objectives.

Microsoft Certified Professional Program

Microsoft certifications provide the best method for proving your command of current Microsoft products and technologies. The exams and corresponding certifications are developed to validate your mastery of critical competencies as you design and develop, or implement and support, solutions with Microsoft products and technologies. Computer professionals who become Microsoft certified are recognized as experts and are sought after throughout the industry. Certification brings various benefits to the individual and to employers and organizations.

> **MORE INFO** **OTHER MICROSOFT CERTIFICATIONS**
>
> For a full list of Microsoft certifications, go to *www.microsoft.com/learning/mcp/default.asp*.

Acknowledgments

This book would not have been possible without my wife's support. She assumed nearly all responsibility for a 9-month-old and a 4-year-old so that I could focus on getting this book written. Ken Jones and Neil Salkind also worked out the details to make the book possible. Even though they didn't offer to do any diaper changes, I'll still thank them anyway.

And the requisite thanks to Tim and Rob from Partners, as well as Jim Oliva and John Eckendorf. Thanks to Bob, Mike, Ernie, and Tim for getting the band back together. It hasn't been that long since I wrote an acknowledgments section, but I can't remember the list of people that I usually thank, so here's to you, person that I can't remember when I'm writing this early on a Sunday morning: consider yourself thanked!

One person I can't forget to thank is you, the reader, not only for reading this acknowledgments section, but also for reading this book. I invite you to contact me, either through my website or on Twitter. Thank you!

Support & Feedback

The following sections provide information on errata, book support, feedback, and contact information.

Errata

We've made every effort to ensure the accuracy of this book and its companion content. Any errors that have been reported since this book was published are listed on our Microsoft Press site at oreilly.com:

http://go.microsoft.com/FWLink/?Linkid=271462

If you find an error that is not already listed, you can report it to us through the same page.

If you need additional support, email Microsoft Press Book Support at *mspinput@ microsoft.com.*

Please note that product support for Microsoft software is not offered through the addresses above.

We Want to Hear from You

At Microsoft Press, your satisfaction is our top priority, and your feedback our most valuable asset. Please tell us what you think of this book at:

http://www.microsoft.com/learning/booksurvey

The survey is short, and we read every one of your comments and ideas. Thanks in advance for your input!

Stay in Touch

Let's keep the conversation going! We're on Twitter: *http://twitter.com/MicrosoftPress.*

Preparing for the Exam

Microsoft certification exams are a great way to build your resume and let the world know about your level of expertise. Certification exams validate your on-the-job experience and product knowledge. Although there is no substitute for on-the-job experience, preparation through study and hands-on practice can help you prepare for the exam. We recommend that you augment your exam preparation plan by using a combination of available study materials and courses. For example, you might use the Exam ref and another study guide for your "at home" preparation, and take a Microsoft Official Curriculum course for the classroom experience. Choose the combination that you think works best for you.

CHAPTER 1

Plan and deploy a server infrastructure

Planning a server infrastructure is key to providing reliable and resilient computing resources to meet business needs. You can attain responsiveness by automating as much as possible in the data center, including such things as server installation and deployment. Virtualization is also an important element in today's data center. Virtual Machine Manager is the tool used for both deployment and management of virtualization infrastructure. Windows Server 2012 enhances File and Storage services to add new features and more security surrounding existing options.

> *important*
> ### Have you read page xviii?
> It contains valuable information regarding the skills you need to pass the exam.

Objectives in this chapter:

- Objective 1.1: Design an automated server installation strategy
- Objective 1.2: Plan and implement a server deployment infrastructure
- Objective 1.3: Plan and implement server upgrade and migration
- Objective 1.4: Plan and deploy Virtual Machine Manager services
- Objective 1.5: Plan and implement file and storage services

Objective 1.1: Design an automated server installation strategy

Providing automation of server installation is important for a responsive, dynamic IT organization. Automation involves creating baseline reference images of servers and then deploying those servers rapidly in response to changing business requirements or to provide additional redundancy. Several tools are available to help with deployments, including tools to create and manage images and a server role for deploying the images onto client or destination computers.

As has been the case in recent versions, Windows Server continues to move toward and feature command-line tools for management alongside the normal Graphical User Interface (GUI) interface. You should be familiar with both the GUI interface and the commands for accomplishing the same task.

Before deploying the servers, you need to design the strategy for supporting the deployments. This means understanding the concepts involved in automated deployment as well as becoming familiar with the tools involved in the process.

This objective covers the following topics:
- Design considerations, including images and bare metal/virtual deployment
- Design of a server implementation using Windows Assessment and Deployment Kit (ADK)
- Design of a virtual server deployment

Understanding design considerations

Choosing an automated server installation strategy involves several design considerations, including the hardware and network infrastructure available for deployment. For example, a lower-bandwidth topology changes the approach. The deployment design chosen also determines how much manual intervention is required to deploy Windows.

When considering a deployment strategy, you should look at the number of machines to be installed. Also consider how many of the machines share the same role and have the same hardware.

An important step in understanding the concepts involved in deployment is learning the components that go into a deployment. Deployment is driven by *image files* that contain the state of a computer, including its operating system and all settings, from a given point in time. You can use several tools in Windows Server 2012 to create images. This chapter concentrates on two: Windows Deployment Services (WDS) and the Windows Assessment and Deployment Kit (ADK).

Three primary phases are involved in Windows deployment: Design, Deployment, and Update.

During the Design phase, you build an initial base or reference image. This is typically accomplished using tools such as WDS, sysprep, or the ADK. Part of the ADK is the Windows System Image Manager (Windows SIM), which assists in working with answer files.

Answer files

XML-formatted answer files provide the settings that you would normally configure when running through a manual installation of Windows. Things such as disk partitioning and network settings can be configured through an answer file so that you don't have to be involved in the setup process for each and every machine deployed. You typically use Windows SIM to create the answer files, but thanks to their XML format, you can edit them with any plain-text editor.

The Deployment phase uses that captured image along with WDS to apply the image to one or more computers in the organization.

An Update and Manage phase enables you to update and manage the images as changes occur to the reference image. During this phase, you can use tools such as Deployment Image Servicing and Management (DISM) and sysprep to edit images.

Images

Windows images contain the information necessary to install a copy of Windows onto another machine. Included in this information are the settings and components specific to the computer onto which the image will be installed.

Two primary types or classes of images are available: boot and install.

BOOT IMAGES

Boot images (boot.wim), used to boot the target computer, include the setup executable as well as the WDS client. Windows DVDs also contain boot.wim files from which other boot images can be built. Boot images are typically added to WDS via the Add Image Wizard by navigating to the source DVD of the operating system. The boot.wim file is normally located in the sources folder of a Windows installation DVD.

Boot images come in two forms: Capture and Discover. Capture images enable the computer to capture an image of itself as a .wim (Windows Image) file. Capture images are typically taken when the computer is fully configured, with all its applications and roles. Once captured, the image is called a *reference* image and should be maintained as needed for environmental changes, such as updates or role and configuration changes.

You create Capture images inside WDS by selecting one of the available boot images and then using the Create Capture Image Wizard. The final step in the Create Capture Image Wizard gives the option to add the Capture Boot Image back to the WDS server, as depicted in Figure 1-1.

FIGURE 1-1 Creating a Capture image and then adding it back to the WDS server.

After a Capture image is created, it can then be deployed to the server by ensuring that the server receiving the image is set to boot from the network with Preboot Execution Environment (PXE). The client can then be captured.

> **NOTE USING SYSPREP**
>
> You must run the sysprep tool on the computer to be captured or it won't be available for image capture. The typical sysprep command is sysprep /generalize /shutdown.

The other boot image type, Discover images, runs the installation setup.exe in WDS mode. This enables the client to locate the WDS server to obtain an install image. Discover images are typically used for client computers that can't use PXE boot or in data center scenarios where PXE might be limited by policy.

INSTALL IMAGES

Install images (install.wim) contain the files customized for the particular image being deployed. WDS can use boot.wim and install.wim from the product DVD during the create-images phase, or it can use customized images for each phase.

DISM can mount both .wim files as well as Virtual Hard Disk (VHD or VHDX) files for servicing. When an image is serviced, you use the Image Capture Wizard to upload it back into the WDS server.

MORE INFO UNDERSTANDING THE DEPLOYMENT PROCESS

See *http://technet.microsoft.com/library/hh825212* for a step-by-step guide to the deployment process.

Windows Deployment Services

The basis for deploying Windows is the Windows Deployment Services role in Windows Server 2012. By default, the Windows Deployment Services role installs two roles: Deployment Server and Transport Server. These roles require a working DHCP server on the network, a DNS server on the network, and an NTFS volume. They also require that the account installing the Windows Deployment Services role be a member of the local administrators group.

NOTE TRANSPORT SERVER ROLE

The Transport Server role is used in environments without Active Directory Domain Services (AD DS), DNS, or DHCP available. The Transport Server role also excludes the WDS image store. The Deployment Server role depends on the Transport Server role, but you can use the Transport Server role as a standalone role.

By default, the DHCP server and the WDS servers run on different machines because WDS communicates with clients using DHCP. However, if DHCP and WDS run on the same computer, you need to add DHCP Option 60 to the DHCP scope on which client computers will communicate with the WDS server. Option 60 enables the client computers to learn about the WDS server in the DHCP response packet.

MORE INFO CONFIGURING DHCP AND WDS

See *http://technet.microsoft.com/library/cc771734* for more information on configuring DHCP and WDS.

In an environment with AD DS, clients can be prestaged. Doing so has the advantage of providing additional security because you can configure the WDS server to respond only to prestaged clients. Computers are *prestaged* (sometimes called *known*) when a computer account is created in the domain for that client computer. An Auto-Add policy option in WDS creates the computer account automatically.

The next objective, "Plan and Implement a Server Deployment Infrastructure," looks closer at WDS.

MORE INFO UNDERSTANDING WDS

See *http://technet.microsoft.com/library/hh831764* for more information on WDS.

Bare metal/virtual deployment

Bare metal or virtual deployments are meant for installations on computers that have no operating system. Computers eligible for bare metal deployment need to be Preboot Execution Environment (PXE) capable, and the network capacity needs to support large transfers.

Deployment to bare metal servers has these general requirements:

- The client computer must be capable of network booting (PXE).
- The client computer must be configured to boot without user interaction.
- You need to create two unattended installation files: one for the WDS screens and one for the setup process itself.

When a client computer boots, it selects a boot image automatically. You can configure this with the following syntax:

```
WDSUTIL /Set-Device /Device:<name> /BootImagePath:<Relative Path>
```

The computer must be prestaged for this to work. Alternatively, you can set a default image globally for all clients on the Boot tab of the WDS server Properties sheet (see Figure 1-2).

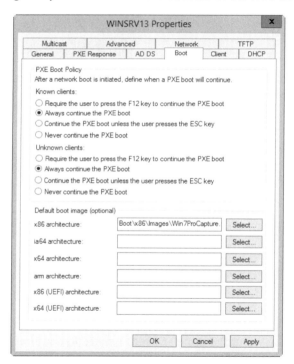

FIGURE 1-2 Use the Boot tab of the WDS server Properties sheet to configure the response to PXE boot requests.

Be conscious not to create a boot loop when planning a virtual deployment. If the computer is configured to boot to the network, it will continue to do so even after the installation takes place, thus continually reinstalling the image. To get around this, configure the hard drive to have higher boot order priority than the network or configure the computer to require F12 to continue booting by using the WDSUTIL /set-server /resetbootprogram:yes command.

The following partitioning schemes are recommended:

For UEFI/GPT Computers:

- Windows RE Tools
- MSR
- Recovery Image
- System
- Windows

For BIOS Computers:

- System
- Windows
- Recovery Image

Using the Windows Assessment and Deployment Kit

The Windows Assessment and Deployment Kit (ADK) provides a rich set of tools for both examining performance and deploying Windows. The assessment pieces help troubleshoot potential problems with hardware and drivers and measure things such as energy and battery usage. The deployment pieces of the ADK combine the Windows OEM Preinstallation Kit and the Windows Automated Installation Kit as well as new tools related to deployment.

EXAM TIP

The Windows ADK creates customized images. Specifically, you should be familiar with the Windows System Image Manager (SIM), the primary tool used by deployment administrators. Windows SIM works with answer files and creates Windows Preinstallation Environment (Windows PE) images. It's these Windows PE images that contain vital information necessary for executing the initial environment for deployment.

Deployments with the ADK involve the following general steps:

1. Create a customized Windows PE.

2. Customize the environment, installing applications and settings for the environment, and then using sysprep to generalize the operating system.

3. Keep the environment up to date.

4. Use the Application Compatibility Toolkit (ACT) to identify application issues.

5. Migrate user data using the User State Migration Tool (USMT).

6. Activate licenses using the Volume Activation Management Toolkit (VAMT).

The sysprep utility takes a computer or image and generalizes it so that it can be re-installed. Sysprep ensures that the computer uses a unique Security Identifier (SID), thus enabling proper licensing and domain functionality. One of the most common problems for deployment and imaging is that sysprep wasn't run on the reference image.

Designing a server implementation with the ADK involves creating an answer file using the Windows SIM. The basic workflow for the SIM is to select a Windows PE image, select a Distribution Share, and then create an answer file.

You select a .wim file by selecting Select Image from the File menu in the Windows SIM. The Windows image shows its contents in the Windows Image pane of the Windows SIM application. If a catalog doesn't yet exist for the image, Windows SIM creates one.

Distribution shares are selected by choosing Select Distribution Share from the File menu. Distribution shares must contain one of the following folders: OEM, Packages, or Out-of-Box Drivers.

After you select the Windows image and distribution share, you can create a basic answer file by using the New Answer File option from the File menu in Windows SIM.

Figure 1-3 shows the Windows SIM interface with a Windows PE image selected, a distribution share selected, and a basic answer file created.

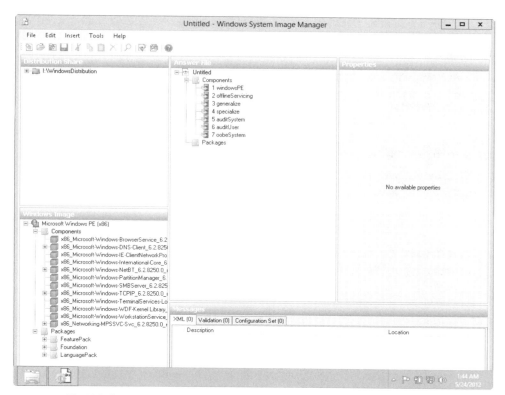

FIGURE 1-3 The Windows System Image Manager.

Packages, in the form of .cab files, can be added to an answer file so that those packages are installed with the image.

MORE INFO **USING WINDOWS ADK TOOLS**

The Windows ADK includes several other tools, such as those for assessments and volume license activation. See *http://technet.microsoft.com/library/hh825486* for more information and a full listing of the tools in the ADK.

Understanding virtual server deployment

Virtual server deployments involve creation of a virtual hard disk (VHD with a .vhd file extension or VHDX with a .vhdx extension) and then deployment of that VHD to another computer. This scenario is called *native boot* because the VHD doesn't require an underlying operating system.

For virtual server deployment, you need to create a VHD using a capture image from a reference computer. The reference computer contains the configuration and applications that you want to clone—in other words, the computer in its pristine state. The image captured from the reference computer can be deployed to other computers, sometimes called *destination computers*.

Some environments use PXE boot with a WDS image. In such an environment, virtual server deployment design can continue using this method rather than the VHD/VHDX method described.

> **MORE INFO** **DEPLOYING A VIRTUAL SERVER FOR NATIVE BOOT**
>
> See *http://technet.microsoft.com/library/dd744338.aspx* for more information on deploying a virtual server for native boot.

THOUGHT EXPERIMENT
Deploying a WDS server

In the following thought experiment, apply what you've learned about this objective. You can find answers to these questions in the "Answers" section at the end of this chapter.

You're deploying a server image and will use WDS for it. As part of the rollout, you have the Deployment Server and Transport Server components installed. A requirement is that the server deploys an image to multiple computers that are all PXE capable.

1. Describe the steps necessary to ensure that the client computers will use the correct image when they're activated, including any configuration that needs to take place on the WDS server.

2. Describe the steps necessary to ensure that the computers can contact the WDS server when they boot.

Objective summary

- Designing an automated server deployment strategy involves several Microsoft tools, including the Windows Assessment and Deployment Kit (ADK) and Windows Deployment Services.
- The ADK creates and manages deployment images, while WDS deploys those images to clients.
- Images come in two forms: boot images and install images.

- Boot images contain information necessary to boot the computer and begin an installation, while install images contain the actual operating system, applications, and other files related to the client being deployed.

- When boot images contain setup information, they're called Discover images. The other type of boot image, Capture images, takes a snapshot of a computer and uses it to create an image file.

Objective review

Answer the following questions to test your knowledge of the information in this objective. You can find the answers to these questions and explanations of why each answer choice is correct or incorrect in the "Answers" section at the end of this chapter.

1. You have a computer configured and need to take an image of it to use as the reference image for deployments. What type of boot image do you need to create to obtain the image?

   A. Preinstallation image

   B. Capture image

   C. Discover image

   D. Virtualization image

2. You have configured a deployment and began the deployment to a client computer and want the client computer to boot from the hard drive after installation. Which command creates this configuration?

   A. wdsutil /set-client /bootdevice:hd

   B. sysprep /client-boot-reset:yes

   C. wdsutil /set-server /resetbootprogram:yes

   D. sysprep /set-client /primaryboot:hd

3. You need to edit an image to change its configuration. The first step is to mount the image. What tool would you use?

   A. Deployment Image Servicing and Management (DISM)

   B. Windows Deployment Services (WDS)

   C. Windows Image Administration

   D. Advanced Image Kit (AIK)

4. When WDS and DHCP operate on the same server, which DHCP option needs to be configured for WDS?

    A. Option 31

    B. Option 60

    C. Boot Option 4

    D. WDS Server Option

Objective 1.2: Plan and implement a server deployment infrastructure

After designing a strategy for automated server installation, you next need to build out the infrastructure to support the server deployment strategy.

This objective covers the following configurations:

- Multicast deployment
- Multisite topology and distribution points
- Multi-server topology
- Autonomous and replica WDS servers

Configuring multicast deployment

WDS supports multicast deployments of server images. With multicast deployments, the image is sent to multiple clients simultaneously, thus using network resources more efficiently.

Multicast deployments are configured within the Windows Deployment Services MMC snap-in. Selecting Create Multicast Transmission within the server section starts the Create Multicast Transmission Wizard, in which you configure the name for the multicast transmission, choose which install image to use, and determine whether to auto-cast or schedule the multicast. Figure 1-4 shows this Multicast Type dialog box.

> *NOTE* **MULTICAST DEPLOYMENTS**
>
> Multicast deployments can be done only on network hardware that supports multicast transmissions.

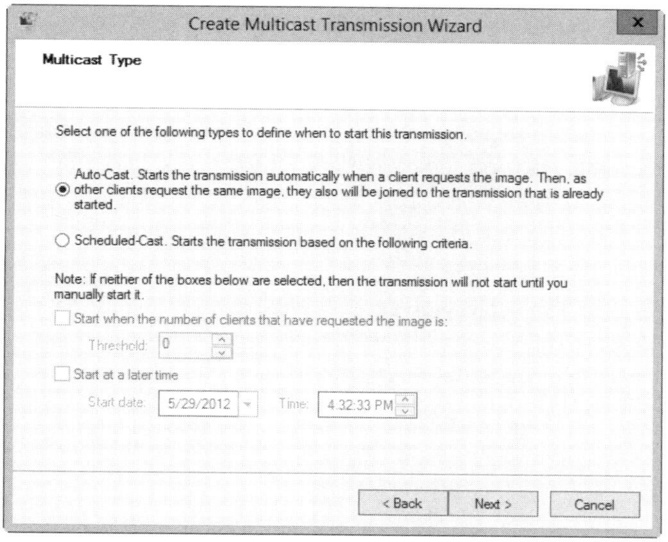

FIGURE 1-4 Configuring the type of multicast to determine when the multicast will occur to clients.

Additional configuration to multicast deployment is achieved within the server's Properties sheet on the Multicast tab, shown in Figure 1-5.

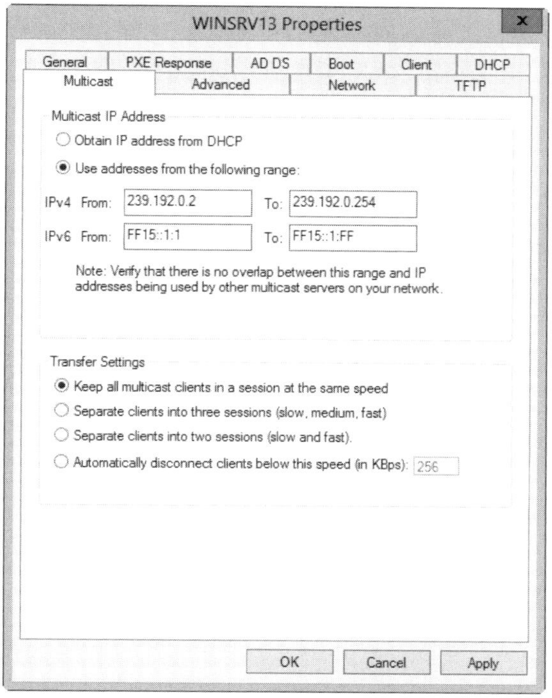

FIGURE 1-5 The Multicast tab within the WDS server Properties sheet.

Configuring multisite topology and distribution points

A multisite topology is typically found in large, geographically dispersed organizations in which the costs of bandwidth and network resources are higher than the management costs associated with maintaining a server at each deployment site. Multisite topologies help make bandwidth consumption more efficient by placing servers closer to the clients serviced by WDS. Each WDS instance runs WDS services and has access to a centralized image store. If client deployments take place over a wide area network (WAN) connection, you should ensure that enough bandwidth is available for deployments.

A multisite topology relies heavily on File Replication Services (FRS) to copy images between WDS servers. Because WDS isn't cluster-aware, the WDS servers don't act in conjunction with one another. However, you can manage disparate WDS servers from a single WDS management console.

The typical scenario for a multisite topology involves prestaging and assigning clients to their nearest or local WDS server (known as a *referral server*).

Prestaging clients

Prestaging clients enables you to specify client settings such as the server that should respond to a deployment request, the boot image, user credentials, and other items. To add a prestaged client, right-click Active Directory Prestaged Devices in the WDS MMC snap-in and select Add Device to launch the Add Prestaged Device Wizard.

The Add Prestaged Device Wizard begins with a dialog box to enter the device name and the device ID. The Device ID is an identifier (GUID, UUID, or MAC address) that enables the WDS server to identify the client when it asks for its deployment (see Figure 1-6).

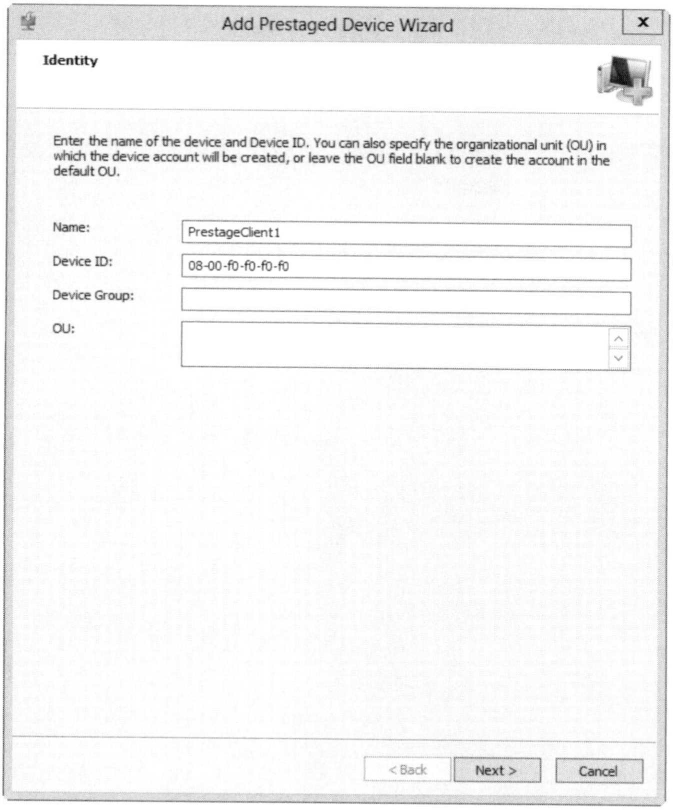

FIGURE 1-6 Prestaging a client in WDS.

Clicking Next brings up the dialog box in Figure 1-7. This dialog box enables you to set the boot information, including the referral server from which the client obtains its installation information. You also can override the server's default PXE Prompt Policy here so that you can deploy servers without needing to press F12 on the server itself to start a PXE boot. The boot image can also be chosen in this dialog box.

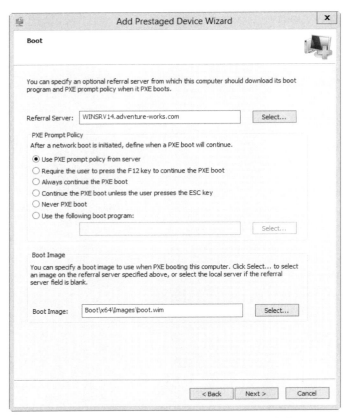

FIGURE 1-7 Choosing boot information for this prestaged client in WDS.

Clicking Next reveals a dialog box in which you can specify the unattended file, as well as create a new unattended installation file (see Figure 1-8).

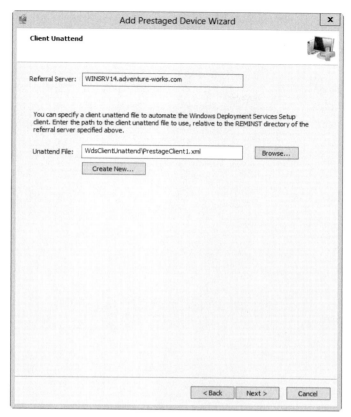

FIGURE 1-8 The Client Unattend dialog box enables you to specify an unattended installation file or create a new one.

Clicking Create New reveals the Create Client Unattend dialog box in Figure 1-9. This important dialog box includes areas to specify the disk partitions for the client, the language to use, and the install image to use for the client.

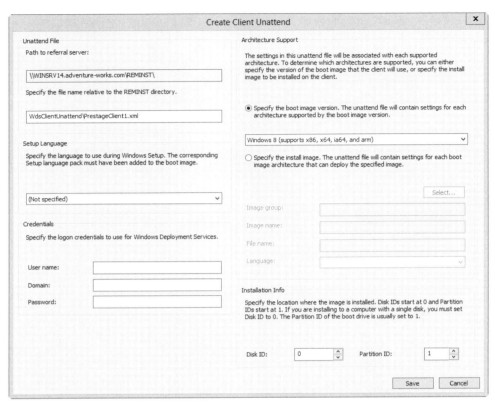

FIGURE 1-9 The Create Client Unattend dialog box enables you to specify a good deal of information about the client to be deployed.

MORE INFO   **USING TYPICAL DEPLOYMENT SCENARIOS**

See *http://technet.microsoft.com/library/hh831764* for more information on typical deployment scenarios.

Configuring a multi-server topology

A multi-server topology helps provide redundancy to the WDS infrastructure and can be used to spread the load image deployment among multiple servers. Like a multisite topology, responses to client deployment requests can be split among the servers by configuring which servers respond to which prestaged clients.

Because WDS isn't cluster-aware and the roles within WDS can't be split among servers, in essence each server operates independently, although sharing a common image store replicated through DFS is typical.

With that in mind, you need to perform limited configuration within WDS in a multi-server topology, aside from configuring the location of the image store with DFS replication.

> **MORE INFO** **UNDERSTANDING DFS REPLICATION**
>
> See *http://technet.microsoft.com/library/jj127250* for more information on DFS replication.

The WDS management console also enables multiple servers to be managed from a central location. Configure this by right-clicking Servers and selecting Add Server. The Add Servers dialog box in Figure 1-10 enables you to choose a server to add to the local management console.

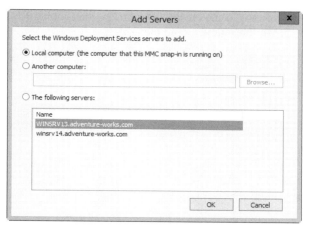

FIGURE 1-10 Choosing a server to manage from the central location helps facilitate a multi-server topology.

Configuring WDS

After the Windows Deployment Services role is installed, you must initialize the server itself. In the WDS Microsoft Management Console (MMC) snap-in, select Configure Server from the server's right-click context menu. In the configuration wizard, set up the mode for the server—Active Directory Domain Services (AD DS) enabled or standalone—as well as how (and whether) to respond to client requests.

If the server is configured with both Deployment Server and Transport Server roles, you can add images to it as the final step in the configuration wizard. If you choose to do so, the Add Image Wizard launches, and you can then select the location where installation media (typically a DVD) can be found.

Most settings in WDS can be reconfigured at any time from within its Properties sheet, which you open by right-clicking the server and selecting Properties from within the Windows Deployment Services MMC snap-in.

Configuring multiple servers to work in tandem involves ensuring that their settings match between servers. For example, the PXE Response Policy, found in the PXE Response tab (see Figure 1-11), sets how WDS responds to PXE requests. If you're deploying multiple servers to be replicas of each other, the settings found in these tabs should match.

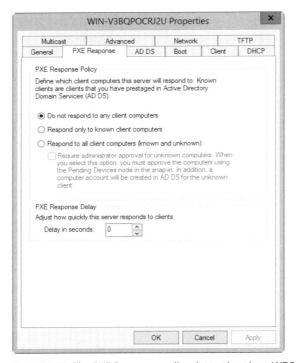

FIGURE 1-11 The PXE Response policy determines how WDS reacts when a PXE request is received.

- **Do Not Respond to Any Client Computers**   Using this setting essentially disables PXE responses from this WDS server.
- **Respond Only to Known Client Computers**   This WDS server responds to prestaged computers. Any unknown client trying to contact the deployment server is placed into the Pending Devices node inside WDS, as shown in Figure 1-12.

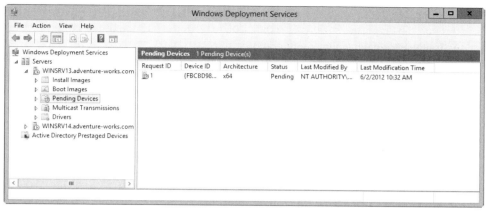

FIGURE 1-12 A pending device in the WDS console.

- **Respond to All Client Computers** The WDS server provides a response to all computers. Notice the check box to enable administrator approval in Figure 1-11.

Figure 1-13 shows the Client tab, which enables you to specify some of the same settings as you could from within the prestaging wizard, such as the location of the unattended file and whether the client will join the domain.

FIGURE 1-13 The Client tab in the WDS server Properties sheet.

EXAM TIP

Click through the Properties sheet tabs within WDS to learn the location of the various options available for deployment configuration.

New for Windows Server 2012 is the ability for WDS to operate as a standalone server, meaning it's not integrated with AD DS. When a server is configured in this Standalone mode, the AD DS tab, among other properties, isn't configurable within the server Properties sheet, as shown in Figure 1-14.

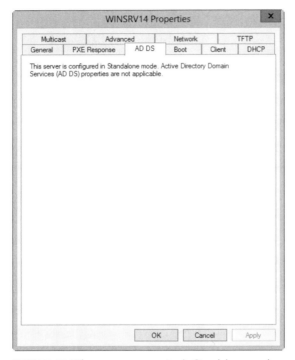

FIGURE 1-14 When a server operates in Standalone mode, some configuration items aren't available.

THOUGHT EXPERIMENT
Configuring a multi-server topology

I n the following thought experiment, apply what you've learned about this objective. You can find answers to these questions in the "Answers" section at the end of this chapter.

You need to configure a multi-server topology so that you can respond to client deployment requests, even if one server goes offline. The overall configuration should be such that clients can request provisioning and have as little intervention as possible. The clients should be joined to the domain automatically and reboot into the operating system.

1. How should you configure the image store for each server (for example, using which tools)?

2. How should the PXE requests be configured for each server?

3. What tools or wizards should you use to automate the process as much as possible?

Objective summary

- Windows Deployment Services is configured at the server level, with the configuration accessed through the Properties sheet.

- Several items can be configured in WDS, including how the server responds to PXE requests, whether the client will join a domain, and how networking such as multicast and DHCP will operate.

- Multicast transmissions are configured with their own wizard accessed through WDS. Multicasting helps conserve bandwidth by deploying the image to multiple clients at the same time.

- Multi-server topologies are used when the number of clients needing to be deployed exceeds the amount that a single server can handle or for redundancy. WDS isn't cluster-aware, and DFS replication is typically used to share images between servers.

- Multisite topologies involve geographically diverse locations in which the cost of bandwidth exceeds the cost of placing and managing a remote server for installs.

- Both multi-server and multisite topologies typically use client prestaging so that clients can be assigned to the correct or closest server.

Objective review

Answer the following questions to test your knowledge of the information in this objective. You can find the answers to these questions and explanations of why each answer choice is correct or incorrect in the "Answers" section at the end of this chapter.

1. Two modes of operation are available when deploying WDS. Which of the following are not included in those modes? (Choose two.)

   A. Deployment

   B. Image Response

   C. Transport

   D. Capture

2. You're deploying Windows Server 2012 using WDS and have multiple locations that need an image, so you need to configure a multisite topology. Which of the following steps is key when working with a multisite topology?

   A. Configuring boot order so that the correct deployment server is chosen

   B. Prestaging the client within WDS on the correct server

   C. Configuring the correct image for the location chosen

   D. Using multicast to ensure the most effective use of bandwidth

3. When creating a Scheduled Cast multicast deployment, with which of the following methods can you begin deployment?

   A. At a future time and/or when a threshold of clients request an image

   B. At a future time and/or when the server comes online

   C. Immediately or at a scheduled time

   D. When the client threshold is set to met or daily

Objective 1.3: Plan and implement server upgrade and migration

Upgrading servers, including changing their roles, and migrating servers from one role to another are necessary tasks for administrators.

This objective covers the following topics:
- Planning for role migration
- Migrating server roles
- Migrating servers across domains and forests

- Designing a server consolidation strategy
- Planning for capacity and resource optimization

Planning for role migration

In general, role migration is defined as upgrades of a server's services from one version of an operating system to another—for example, from Windows Server 2008 to Windows Server 2012. Migration planning depends primarily on the roles you need to migrate. Migrating AD DS requires different planning and execution than migrating File Services or other roles. Migrations retain settings and configuration and can be used to move from physical to virtualized installations of Windows.

Because Windows Server 2012 is x64-based architecture, you can migrate only from x64-based servers. If the server isn't x64-based, migration isn't possible and the server will need to have a clean install, after which the role can be configured for that server.

Windows Server Migration Tools provide a set of Windows PowerShell cmdlets to facilitate the migration of roles. You can install these as a Feature in Windows Server 2012. Windows Server Migration Tools can be used to migrate between the following editions of Windows Server:

- Windows Server Foundation
- Windows Server Standard
- Windows Server Enterprise
- Windows Server Datacenter

The Windows Server Migration Tools are added to the Windows PowerShell command line with the following command:

```
Add-PSSnapin Microsoft.Windows.ServerManager.Migration
```

After that snap-in is added, the migration-related cmdlets are available, specific to the type of migration being performed. As previously stated, planning for migration depends largely on what roles are being migrated. However, some steps are common to all role migration planning:

- Identifying source and destination servers
- Installing all critical updates to the source server
- Ensuring that both the source and destination servers have the same number of network adapters
- Preparing a migration store file location that source and destination servers can both access

There are also tasks related to specific roles. The following planning steps are involved in select role migration scenarios.

Planning migration of AD DS and DNS

1. Introduce Windows Server 2012 into the domain so that the existing forest and domain are prepared.

2. Ensure that the destination server meets the hardware requirements for the hosting Active Directory roles.

3. Create an Active Directory backup of the source server.

4. Install Windows on the destination server, using a temporary name and IP address because both will be changed later.

5. Ensure that the source DNS server is running correctly, as discussed in the "Migrating server roles" section.

Planning migration of File Services servers

1. Install Windows on the destination server.

2. Ensure that the time and date are synchronized with the source server.

3. Match the same File Services features on both the source and destination servers.

4. Open TCP and UDP port 7000 on any network resources or firewalls between the source and destination servers.

5. Verify that the destination server has enough free disk space and that any quotas allow the free space to be used for storage.

> **MORE INFO**   **UNDERSTANDING ROLE MIGRATION**
>
> See *http://technet.microsoft.com/library/jj134202.aspx* for more information on role migration and Windows Server Migration Tools.

Migrating server roles

After you plan how the migration will take place and perform initial steps for the migration, you need to perform the actual migration. Like the planning stage, the steps involved in performing the actual migration vary according to the type of migration being performed. This section examines migration scenarios for common roles.

Migrating AD DS and DNS server roles

1. Add the Active Directory Domain Services role to the destination server.

2. Record the DNS settings on the source server using ipconfig /all.

3. Replicate the source server's DNS settings onto the destination server. Use the Dns-Service.REG and Dns-Software.REG files, which should be copied to %windir%\System32\DNS on the destination server.

4. Execute the DNSconvergeCheck.cmd Convergence Verification Script to ensure that all DNS records are replicated between the source and destination servers.

5. Ensure that the Flexible Single Master Operations (FSMO) roles are migrated, if necessary.

6. Migrate IP addresses by changing the source server's IP to a different IP address and then changing the destination server to the source server's original IP.

7. Rename the source server and use the netdom renamecomputer command to give the destination server the source server's original name.

8. Verify that the destination server is operating as the new domain controller.

Migrating File Services roles

1. Freeze configuration on the source server.

2. Migrate settings such as server message block (SMB), Offline Files (also called *client-side caching* or CSC), DFS Namespaces, DFS Replication, File Server Resource Manager (FSRM), and Shadow Copies of Shared Folders.

3. Export local users and groups. From the Windows Migration Tools PowerShell, use this command:

```
Export-SmigServerSetting -User All -Group -Path <storepath>
```

4. Import the users from the source to the destination server:

   ```
   Import-SmigServerSetting -User All -Group -Path <storepath>
   ```

5. Migrate the data.

   > **MORE INFO** **MIGRATING DATA**
   >
   > See *http://technet.microsoft.com/library/dd379474%28v=ws.10%29#BKMK_MigrateData*
   > for more information on this step as it applies to your environment.

6. Rename and re-address the source server by changing its name and IP address.

7. Reconfigure the destination server to have the same name and address as the source.

8. Import settings from Step 2 to the destination server.

Migrating Dynamic Host Configuration Protocol (DHCP) server roles

1. Install the DHCP role onto the destination server.

2. Stop the DHCP Server service (Stop-Service DHCPserver).

3. Collect data from the source server with the Migration Tool cmdlet Export-SmigServerSetting:

   ```
   Export-SmigServerSetting -featureID DHCP -User All -Group -IPConfig -path
   <storepath>
   ```

4. Delete the DHCP authorization on the source DHCP server:

   ```
   Netsh DHCP delete server <server FQDN> <Server IP Address>
   ```

5. On the destination server, run the cmdlet Import-SmigServerSetting:

   ```
   Import-SmigServerSetting -featureID DHCP -User All -Group -IPConfig <All | Global
   | NIC> -SourcePhysicalAddress <Source IP Address> -TargetPhysicalAddress -Force
   -path <storepath>
   ```

6. Start the DHCP service on the destination server:

   ```
   Start-Service DHCPServer
   ```

7. Authorize the destination server (case sensitive):

   ```
   netsh DHCP add server <Server FQDN> <Server IP Address>
   ```

Migrating servers across domains and forests

Server migration can occur across domains and forests, although you can't migrate some roles that depend on AD DS. Reasons for migrating domains and forests include organizational changes, mergers, and consolidation of regional locations. The Active Directory Migration Tool (ADMT) facilitates migration of objects across domains and across forests. Migrating objects between forests is known as an *inter*forest migration; migrating objects between domains within the same forest is known as *intra*forest migration.

A trust relationship is typically created for both interforest and intraforest migration. The trust enables ADMT to migrate computer resources between domains. Interforest trusts are called *Forest Trusts* and can be a one-way trust or a two-way transitive trust.

> **MORE INFO**   **UNDERSTANDING AND CREATING FOREST TRUSTS**
>
> See *http://technet.microsoft.com/library/cc772440* for more information on Forest Trusts and *http://technet.microsoft.com/library/cc754626* for a step-by-step guide to creating a Forest Trust.

Domain Trusts come in various forms and with various transitive properties. These include external trusts for domains between forests, shortcut trusts that exist between domains within a forest, and realm trusts for relationships between Active Directory domains and non-Windows Kerberos version 5 (V5) realms.

> **MORE INFO**   **UNDERSTANDING TRUST TYPES**
>
> See *http://technet.microsoft.com/library/cc771568* for information on the different types of trusts, including when to use each type.

ADMT migrates computers between domains and forests after a trust is established. Each computer requires a restart after moving between domains, so this should be accounted for when planning migration.

> **MORE INFO**   **USING ADMT**
>
> See *http://techhnet.microsoft.com/library/cc974412* for more information on using ADMT.

Designing a server consolidation strategy

The term *server consolidation* typically means virtualization with technology such as Hyper-V, although that's not always the case. Server consolidation can also mean consolidation of roles from multiple servers onto one server. When considering this latter form of consolidation, you must consider how consolidation of services will affect infrastructure reliability. For example, you don't want to place too many services or roles onto one server in case that server goes down. Therefore, providing redundancy and separation of services to ensure uptime and reliability is key when designing server consolidation.

Server consolidation by virtualization involves several steps:

1. Determine the virtualization scope.

2. Create a list of workloads.

3. Select backup and fault-tolerance approaches.

4. Summarize and analyze workload requirements.

> **MORE INFO** **USING THE WINDOWS SERVER VIRTUALIZATION GUIDE**
>
> More information about these steps and additional steps that involve execution of the strategy can be found in the Windows Server Virtualization Guide at *http://technet.microsoft .com/library/bb897507.aspx.*

Determine the virtualization scope

The first step in designing a server consolidation strategy involves defining the scope of the project. For example, virtualizing an entire datacenter at once can be risky, as can the initial investment. Also, if the organization has multiple data centers, each might need to have virtualization hardware installed, which increases the initial cost of deployment. However, deployment to those remote locations can in fact provide good pilot projects for the overall virtualization deployment.

Create a list of workloads

Creating a list of workloads involves documenting what applications are currently deployed, their current location, what operating system those applications use, the resources requirements for the workload, and the administrator or person responsible for the application or workload.

The compatibility of the workload, specifically the ability for that application or workload to be virtualized, should also be undertaken at this time. If a given workload isn't compatible or supported on virtualized infrastructure, it must be accounted for and excluded from the consolidation strategy. This task includes not only the technical compatibility but also the vendor's support and licensing model compatibility when running in a virtualized environment.

DETERMINING RESOURCE REQUIREMENTS

Determining the resource requirements for the virtualized workloads is an important facet when creating a list of workloads. You should measure the current resources for physical machines and workloads, and then add resources to ensure that the load doesn't meet its peak load immediately on being virtualized.

Table 1-1 lists three options for determining resource requirements.

TABLE 1-1 Options for determining resource requirements

Option	Description
Microsoft Assessment and Planning Toolkit (MAP)	Inventories current environment and creates virtualization assessments. This option uses Windows Management Instrumentation (WMI), is free, and produces a Microsoft Excel spreadsheet.
System Center Virtual Machine Manager	Analyzes resource requirements. Requires an agent to be installed on the server being analyzed. This option also incurs licensing costs but produces a graphical report.
Manually	You can also gather statistics manually using benchmarking, performance counters, and specifications from vendors or developers. Typically uses Performance Monitor (perfmon).

SELECTING BACKUP AND FAULT-TOLERANCE APPROACHES

Table 1-2 identifies three options for backups.

TABLE 1-2 Backup options

Backup Method	Description
Application Backup	Simplified process with smaller file size but can negatively affect performance while backup is being taken.
Workload Backup	Backs up virtualized workload via Windows backup or System Center. This approach can have negative performance implications while the backup is being taken.
Virtualization Host Backup	Backups can be taken of the entire virtual machine, both offline and online. Offline causes the virtual machine to be turned off and thus involves downtime. An online backup uses System Center Data Protection Manager and takes a snapshot using Volume Shadow Copy Service (VSS) and does not involve downtime.

Fault tolerance for virtualized hosts has three options, as shown in Table 1-3.

TABLE 1-3 Fault-tolerance options for virtualized hosts

Fault-Tolerance Method	Description
Network load balancing	Applications such as web servers are good candidates for this approach because they are stateless and don't need to maintain connections with clients.
Application-specific clustering	Applications such as SQL Server have built-in cluster capabilities, which can be used in a virtualized environment.
Host clustering	Microsoft Failover Cluster Service can be used to configure failover clustering when shared storage is used.

Summarize and analyze workload requirements

So far you've collected a great deal of information about your organization's infrastructure. This phase involves analyzing all that information to determine how best to virtualize the workloads involved.

In this phase, you look at how workloads can be grouped, keeping in mind that regulatory requirements might prevent workloads from being virtualized in the same datacenter or other requirements might deploy workloads at different locations.

Also during this phase, you gather actual resource requirements such as CPU, memory, disk (both capacity and performance), and network. The goal is to summarize those requirements so that you can plan what types and capacities are necessary to virtualize the workloads.

Planning for capacity and resource optimization

Many of the same processes involved when planning for virtualization can be used for capacity and resource optimization. Several approaches are identified for capacity and resource optimization. For example, tools such as workload analysis with the Microsoft Assessment and Planning (MAP) toolkit are key to optimizing resource usage. Also, Windows Server 2012 introduces new items related to capacity optimization: data deduplication and trim storage. This section discusses each option.

The MAP toolkit

The MAP toolkit provides several reports useful for capacity planning and resource optimization. MAP primarily uses Windows Management Instrumentation (WMI) to collect information, although some tests access the remote registry.

The MAP toolkit uses various discovery methods, including

- **AD DS**   Examines computer objects that are in AD DS but is limited to computers that appear in AD DS. As a result, Linux and other computers might not show up.

- **Imported and manual**   Means computers are either imported from a file or entered manually.

- **Scan by IP Address range**   Scans up to 100,000 IPs to discover computers.

- **System Center Configuration Manager (SCCM)**   Discovers computers managed by SCCM.

- **Windows Network Protocols**   Use the WIN32 LAN Manager Application Programming Interface (API) to search for computers available through the Computer Browser service.

The MAP toolkit uses various means to collect inventory information on computers under its purview. For example, the MAP toolkit can use Secure Shell (SSH) to collect information from computers running Linux as well as various APIs for other vendors.

MAP does much more than resource optimization, but this task concentrates solely on using MAP for assessment of underutilized resources. Before using MAP, you should ensure that the environment meets the following criteria:

- Firewall software allows WMI traffic from the inventory subnet.
- Remote Administration and File and Printer Sharing are allowed through firewalls relevant between the inventory subnet and the computers to be inventoried.
- Network access policy for local accounts should be set to Classic mode, if necessary.

MAP contains several helpful wizards to assist in the inventory process:

- Inventory and Assessment Wizard
- Performance Metrics Wizard
- Hardware Library Wizard
- Server Virtualization and Consolidation Wizard
- Prepare New Reports and Proposals Wizard

The following are recommended for performance data collection:

- A minimum of two days' worth of performance data, with seven days recommended, should be used.
- Performance collection should be run during peak times, such as heavy end-of-month or quarterly activities.
- Don't leave long gaps between performance collections.

The Inventory and Assessment Wizard is used frequently to determine readiness for upgrades.

> **MORE INFO   USING MAP**
>
> See the Microsoft Assessment and Planning Toolkit page on TechNet at *http://technet .microsoft.com/library/bb977556.aspx* for more information, including a Getting Started Guide, which provides specific information on using MAP.

Trim storage

Windows Server 2012 has two new features, data deduplication and trim storage, that assist with capacity optimization. Data deduplication is discussed in Objective 1.5, "Plan and implement file and storage services."

> **NOTE   TRIM STORAGE**
>
> Trim storage was previously available with certain disk configurations for Windows 7.

Trim storage reclaims unused storage space. A typical use case for trim storage surrounds its use in SAN environments with virtual machine disk space, in which the virtual machine can be configured to use 100GB temporarily but in reality is only using 10GB most of the time. Trim storage enables you to reconfigure the disk allocation so that the SAN won't reserve that temporary 100GB of space but instead trims down to its normal 10GB of usage, thus reclaiming all that extra space.

Trim storage offers an Application Programming Interface (API) that enables applications to return storage and also performs a scheduled optimization pass to consolidate storage.

> **MORE INFO**   **UNDERSTANDING TRIM STORAGE**
>
> See *http://technet.microsoft.com/library/hh831391* for more information on trim storage.

THOUGHT EXPERIMENT
Designing a backup and fault-tolerance method

In the following thought experiment, apply what you've learned about this objective. You can find answers to these questions in the "Answers" section at the end of this chapter.

You're designing a backup and fault-tolerance method for virtualized hosts. The servers involved are domain members, and their main role is to run Internet Information Services to serve web pages. You want to enable one machine to handle incoming requests in case the other server becomes unavailable or goes offline.

1. Which fault-tolerance method would you choose and why?
2. Which backup method is most appropriate for this role in this configuration?

Objective summary

- Planning for server migration typically means upgrading servers from older versions of Windows Server to the latest version.
- The source server involved in a migration must be backed up before beginning server migration.
- The steps involved in server migration depend largely on the role involved, although the planning of any server migration involves common steps.
- The Windows Server Migration Tools assist in server migration.
- Capacity and resource optimization is pursued through different means. Windows Server 2012 introduced trim storage to assist in capacity optimization, and you can use the Microsoft Assessment and Planning (MAP) toolkit to produce reports of resource utilization.

Objective review

Answer the following questions to test your knowledge of the information in this objective. You can find the answers to these questions and explanations of why each answer choice is correct or incorrect in the "Answers" section at the end of this chapter.

1. This objective identified four steps involved in planning for server virtualization. Which of the following is not one of those steps?

   A. Determine the virtualization scope.

   B. Summarize and analyze workload requirements.

   C. Create a list of workloads.

   D. Optimize workload resources.

2. What is a domain trust between forests called?

   A. External trust

   B. Forest trust

   C. Forest-level domain trust

   D. IntraService trust

3. The Windows Server Migration Tools are added with which command?

   A. Add-Snapin Microsoft.Windows.ServerManager.Migration

   B. Add-PSSnapin Microsoft.Windows.ServerManager.Migration

   C. PSS-Snapin Microsoft.Windows.Tools.Migration

   D. Add-PSS Microsoft.Windows.Migration

4. Along with the remote registry server, the MAP toolkit typically uses which type of communication to collect information?

   A. SSH

   B. Remote API

   C. SMB

   D. WMI

5. How many days of data collection is recommended for performance reports?

   A. 14

   B. 4

   C. 30

   D. 7

Objective 1.4: Plan and deploy Virtual Machine Manager services

Virtual Machine Manager (VMM), part of System Center 2012, enables centralized management of virtualized workloads. Included in this management is the capability to work with networking and storage for virtual machines. Because virtualization is a central feature of most datacenters, using VMM is a key skill for enterprise administrators. This objective assumes that you have VMM installed and configured.

> **MORE INFO** **UNDERSTANDING VMM CONFIGURATION**
>
> If you're not familiar with creation of virtual machine (VM) templates and other aspects of VMM configuration, see *http://technet.microsoft.com/library/gg610610.aspx* to gain some perspective before reading through the coverage here.

This objective covers the following topics:

- Designing VMM service templates
- Defining operating system profiles
- Configuring hardware and capability profiles
- Managing services
- Configuring image and template libraries
- Managing local networks

Designing VMM service templates

Services, in the sense of virtual machines, are collections of virtual machines deployed together to provide an application. Central to this concept are tiers or a tier-based infrastructure in which multiple tiers provide the service and an individual tier has the configuration necessary for its portion of the service.

VMM service templates contain information about the service as a whole, including all tiers. VMM service templates are created and managed with the Service Template Designer, which is accessed through the VMs and Services workspace in the VMM Console.

Before using Service Template Designer, you should become familiar with creating Logical Networks, VM Templates, and other pieces of the given service template necessary for its configuration. Also, users creating service templates must be administrators or have the Author action in their user role scopes.

MORE INFO **CREATING SERVICES AND SERVICE TEMPLATES**

See *http://technet.microsoft.com/library/hh427290* for more information on the prerequisites for creating services and service templates.

When Service Template Designer is launched, you can choose from certain predefined templates, called patterns, including single-, two-, and three-tier templates, or you can choose a blank template (see Figure 1-15).

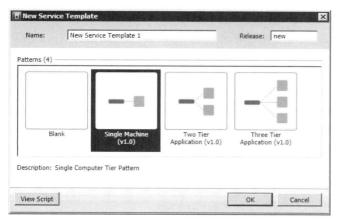

FIGURE 1-15 Choosing a Single Machine Tier pattern in Service Template Designer.

Service Template Designer then presents a template based on your pattern selection. In the case of Figure 1-15, a Single Machine template was chosen; Figure 1-16 shows the template in Service Template Designer.

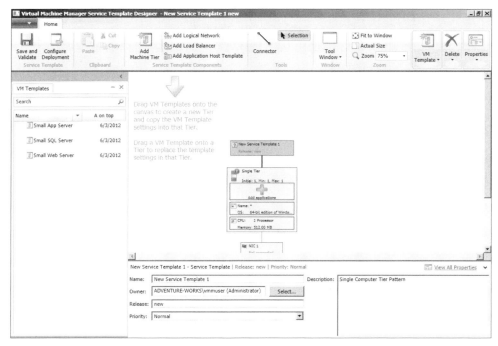

FIGURE 1-16 A Single Machine Tier template in Service Template Designer.

Service templates are created according to the specification you have for the service. You can drag additional VM templates onto the canvas and add them to the template as needed. Figure 1-16 shows three VM templates defined (they were predefined outside Service Template Designer). You could drag these onto the canvas and add them to the service template being designed.

Double- or right-clicking a given tier reveals the Properties sheet for that tier, in which you can configure the tier's properties. For example, Figure 1-17 shows that a Virtual Hard Disk was added, which is a requirement for the Single Tier application template. You also need to connect the predefined templates to a domain, which you accomplish also within the tier properties.

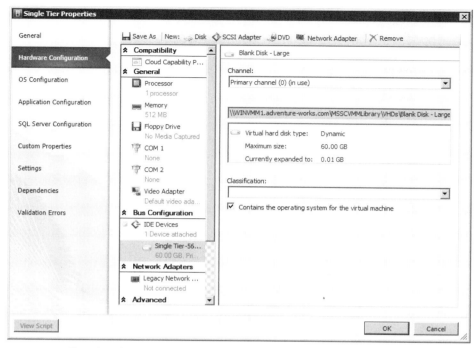

FIGURE 1-17 Changing the hardware configuration of a Single Tier template in Service Template Designer.

Connecting the host to a logical network is another requirement when creating a service template. You do this with the Add Logical Network component in Service Template Designer, and then use the Connector tool to connect the logical network to the network interface in the tier. The logical network component also must be associated with a logical network through its properties. In the case of Figure 1-18, the logical network is associated with Logical Network 1, which was predefined by the author.

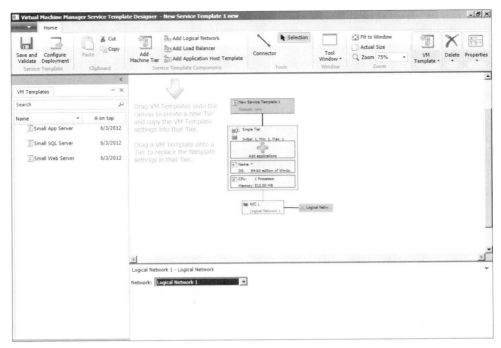

FIGURE 1-18 Associating a logical network with a tier.

When you've made changes to the template, click Save and Validate. Service Template Designer then examines the configuration and looks for potential problems. When you're ready to deploy the template, choose Configure Deployment from the toolbar. VMM then tries to place the service by examining the template and looking for available hosts on which to deploy the virtual host. This process includes examining the resources requested for the service template and comparing those against the available resources.

You can set service template properties through the canvas at the template level, including such properties as the name of the service template itself, its release number or version name, and who has access to deploy using the service template. You also can change tier properties including the tier name, the capability to scale or add machines to a deployed service, the service group or upgrade domain, the hardware, guest OS, application, and SQL Server configuration. You can also configure networking objects through the canvas in Service Template Designer.

For example, you might need to deploy additional virtual machines to a service tier to handle additional load. To scale a service out, the service template needs to allow scaling. This aspect is configured through Service Template Designer. Unless you have a business reason for not allowing scaling on a given tier, you should allow the tier to be scaled by checking the This Computer Tier Can Be Scaled Out check box and increasing the Maximum Instance Count accordingly. Also, increase the upgrade domains at the same time to enable VMM to minimize service downtime for later upgrades.

> **MORE INFO**   **SCALING OUT A SERVICE**
>
> See *http://technet.microsoft.com/library/gg675080* for step-by-step instructions on scaling out a service.

Another task related to service templates is adding a tier. You can add a service tier in two ways: by dragging a virtual machine template onto the canvas or by using the Create Machine Tier Template Wizard. In practice, however, adding a tier to an existing service template is less common than creating a new template to handle the additional tier.

> **MORE INFO**   **ADDING TIERS AND USING SERVICE TEMPLATE DESIGNER**
>
> See *http://technet.microsoft.com/library/hh410345* for a step-by-step guide to adding a tier. See *http://technet.microsoft.com/library/gg650474.aspx* for more information on using Service Template Designer overall.

Defining operating system profiles

Operating system profiles are used to create standardized virtual machines. You can define operating system profiles in two ways: by using the Create New Guest OS Profile manually or by using a wizard within the New Template Wizard.

Creating a new standalone guest operating system profile

In VMM, you define operating system profiles in the library by clicking Create and then clicking New Guest OS Profile. Doing so begins the New Guest OS Profile dialog box (see Figure 1-19).

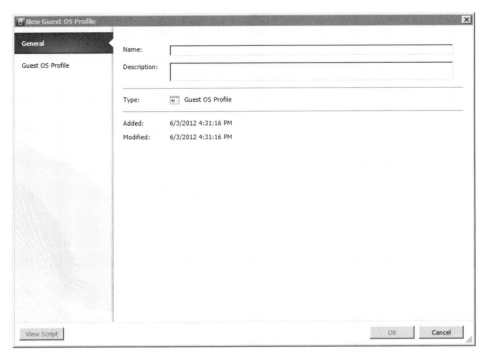

FIGURE 1-19 Creating a new standalone guest operating system profile.

You configure the main settings for the profile in the Guest OS Profile pane of the New Guest OS Profile dialog box. Within this pane you can configure the computer name, administrator password, product key, time zone, and operating system to be used when this profile is used to create a virtual machine. Roles and features to be auto-installed are configured, as are the joining of a domain and pointing to a script file, among other settings. Figure 1-20 shows this pane.

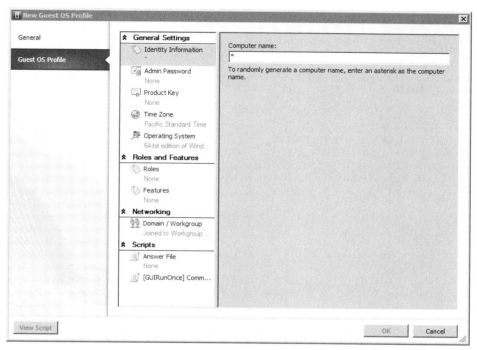

FIGURE 1-20 The Guest OS Profile pane enables the configuration of a guest operating system profile.

Defining a guest operating system profile with template creation

You can also define a guest operating system profile when creating a template via the Create VM Template Wizard. Doing so reveals a configuration page for the operating system profile that is similar to that found when creating a standalone profile. Figure 1-21 depicts the guest operating system profile definition as part of the Create VM Template Wizard.

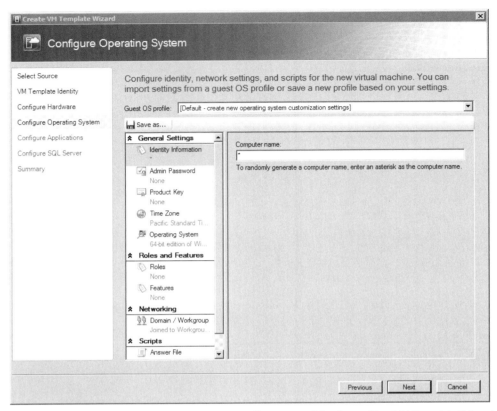

FIGURE 1-21 Creating a guest operating system profile as part of the Create New VM Template Wizard.

Configuring hardware and capability profiles

Hardware and capability profiles are library resources such as processors and memory that are available for a virtual machine. As library resources, both types of capabilities are defined within the Library workspace in the VMM Administrator. The properties for existing capability profiles also are accessed within the Library workspace.

Capability profiles are frequently used to ensure that a virtual machine or service uses a minimum number or amount of a resource. For example, Figure 1-22 shows the Create Capability Profile Wizard, in which a minimum number of network adapters are required.

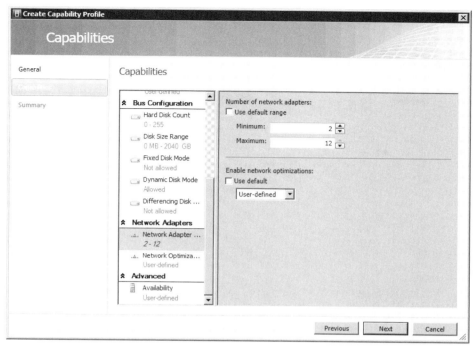

FIGURE 1-22 Defining a minimum number of network adapters with a capability profile.

You can also use Capability Profiles to define whether a virtual machine is created on a high availability cluster. Capability Profiles are edited within the Library section by selecting Properties.

Virtual Machine Manager has three built-in Capability Profiles: Hyper-V, XenServer, and ESX Server. The definition of each profile reflects the different capabilities inherent in each respective platform. For example, the XenServer profile allows only a maximum of 32GB of memory, whereas the Hyper-V profile can use up to 64GB.

Hardware profiles store specific hardware information rather than ranges as with Capability Profiles. For example, Figure 1-23 illustrates a Hardware profile being configured to use a specific type of SCSI Adapter. This might be used in a case where the application requires a certain type of adapter.

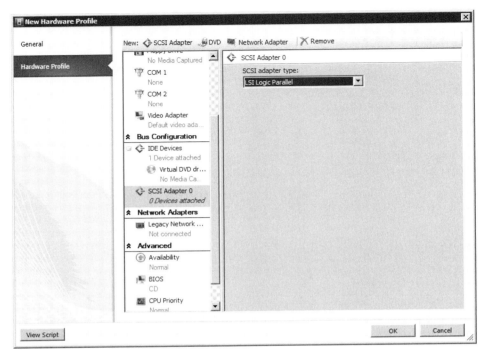

FIGURE 1-23 Creating a hardware profile in VMM.

Managing services

After a service is deployed, you can manage it through its lifecycle. You can make changes to a deployed service in two ways:

- Update the existing virtual machines
- Deploy new, updated virtual machines

Updating existing virtual machines for smaller changes is recommended because it's a less time-consuming process than deploying new virtual machines. Deploy new virtual machines when you need to make a larger change to the environment, such as install a service pack to a guest operating system.

> **MORE INFO   UPDATING AND APPLYING SERVICE TEMPLATES**
>
> See *http://technet.microsoft.com/library/gg675120* for a step-by-step procedure for updating a service template and for information on applying updates to a deployed service.

Configuring image and template libraries

Image and template libraries are configured and managed through the Library workspace in the VMM console. To add images (such as a VHD file) to VMM, choose Create Host Profile from the Library workspace. In the New Host Profile Wizard, you can import the VHD image and set other configuration pertinent to the host profile you're creating. Figure 1-24 shows an example of the New Host Profile Wizard.

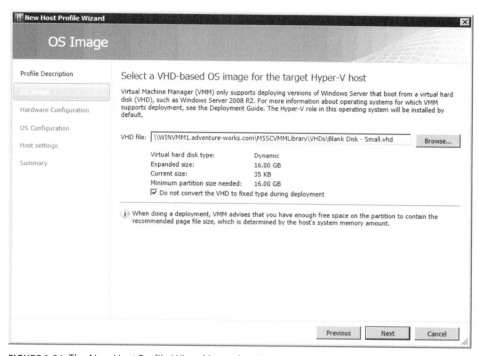

FIGURE 1-24 The New Host Profile Wizard is used to import an image into VMM.

Templates are also managed within the Library workspace, as shown in Figure 1-25.

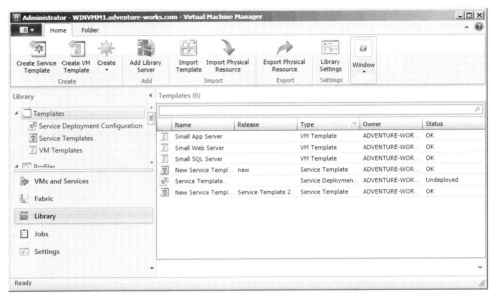

FIGURE 1-25 The Template Library in VMM is the starting point for configuration of templates.

MORE INFO   CREATING VIRTUAL MACHINE TEMPLATES AND HOST PROFILES

See *http://technet.microsoft.com/library/hh427282* for information on creating a virtual machine template and *http://technet.microsoft.com/library/gg610653.aspx* for information on creating host profiles.

Managing logical networks

The Fabric workspace in VMM enables you to create and configure logical networks. To manage a logical network, you right-click and select Properties. In the logical network's Properties sheet, you can change the Name and Network Site properties. Figure 1-26 shows the Network Site pane of the logical network Properties sheet.

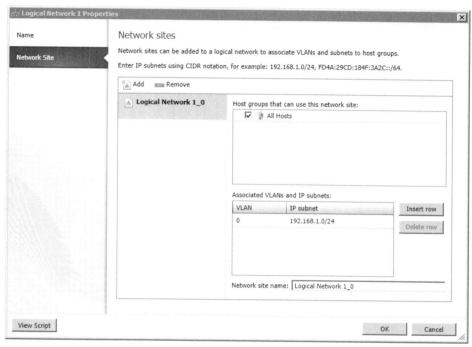

FIGURE 1-26 The Network Site pane of the logical network Properties sheet.

The Network Site pane is where you can associate VLANs and subnets with host groups. A typical scenario is to create logical networks for traffic isolation. For example, you might create logical networks to mirror those in the physical network such as a network outside the firewall, in the main core of the data center, or a network for management and backups to assist in management and separation of virtual machines.

> **NOTE   NETWORK SITES**
>
> You'll sometimes see a logical network referred to as a *network site*.

The scenario depicted in Figure 1-26 associates a VLAN and IP subnet with the logical network, although this is required only if you have static IP pools to be managed by VMM. If DHCP is in use, you don't have to associate any VLANs or IP subnets, but you can still define a VLAN (if applicable) while using DHCP.

Defining static IP pools

You can configure static IP pools in the Create Static IP Address Pool Wizard. Within the wizard you configure the network site, including its subnet and VLAN, default gateway, DNS servers, WINS servers, and other reserved IP settings. Figure 1-27 shows the Create Static IP Address Pool Wizard.

FIGURE 1-27 The Create Static IP Address Pool Wizard in VMM.

MORE INFO   **USING IP ADDRESS POOLS AND LOGICAL NETWORKS**

See *http://technet.microsoft.com/library/gg610590* for more information on how to create IP address pools and *http://technet.microsoft.com/library/gg610596* for more information on logical networks.

THOUGHT EXPERIMENT
Scaling out a tier

In the following thought experiment, apply what you've learned about this objective. You can find answers to these questions in the "Answers" section at the end of this chapter.

You now have a deployed service template running a single-tier virtual machine. You recently found that this server can't keep up with the load being imposed on it. Therefore, you want to scale out the tier but discover that the service template doesn't allow scaling out.

1. How should you solve this?

2. What steps should you take in Service Template Designer to ensure that this doesn't occur in the future?

Objective summary

- Virtual Machine Manager is a powerful application for configuration and deployment of virtual machines.
- VMM has several workspaces used to define and configure virtual machines and their resources. Among these are the Libraries and Fabric workspaces.
- Use operating system profiles to define the resources available for a virtual machine.
- Use service templates to create complex, multi-tiered services that you can then deploy across virtual resources. Doing so helps maximize resource usage while minimizing effort and providing redundancy.
- Use logical networks to connect virtual machines to physical network interfaces. You can also use logical networks to create configurations so that multi-tiered services can communicate.

Objective review

Answer the following questions to test your knowledge of the information in this objective. You can find the answers to these questions and explanations of why each answer choice is correct or incorrect in the "Answers" section at the end of this chapter.

1. Which tool is used to edit or change service templates?
   - **A.** Service Template Designer
   - **B.** Virtual Service Editor
   - **C.** Service Resource Library
   - **D.** Virtual Template Designer

2. Logical networks are managed through which workspace?
   - **A.** Resources
   - **B.** Library
   - **C.** Fabric
   - **D.** Network Services

3. Which type of profile can you use to determine whether a machine is deployed to be highly available?
   - **A.** Capability
   - **B.** Hardware
   - **C.** Fabric
   - **D.** Availability

Objective 1.5: Plan and implement file and storage services

File and storage services have evolved since the days of locally installed hard drives. Most enterprises use Fibre Channel Storage Area Networks (SANs). Windows Server 2012 enables several complex file and storage scenarios to take advantage of the maturation of virtualization technologies.

This objective covers the following topics:

- Planning considerations for iSCSI SANs, Fibre Channel SANs, Virtual Fibre Channel, Storage Spaces, storage pools, and data deduplication
- How to configure the iSCSI Target Server
- How to configuring Internet Storage Name Server (iSNS)
- How to configuring Network File System (NFS)
- How to installing Device-Specific Modules (DSMs)

Planning for file and storage service

Windows Server 2012 extends the multitude of available file and storage options. System Center 2012 Data Protection Manager (DPM) further adds to the options for providing redundancy for data and storage.

Direct Attached Storage (DAS) is still used, although enterprise installations frequently use Fibre Channel Storage Area Networks (SANs) to provide block-level access to disk resources. Network Attached Storage (NAS) is also used to provide file-level access to data. You can connect NAS devices directly to the network, where they frequently use the Server Message Block (SMB) protocol when connecting to Windows-based computers.

iSCSI and Fibre Channel

Internet SCSI (iSCSI) is another method of providing SCSI-based access to block-level file systems. iSCSI varies from Fibre Channel SCSI in that data is transferred via the existing IP network versus a separate Fibre Channel network. Windows Server 2012 provides an iSCSI Target Server role.

Several advantages for iSCSI SANs are as follows:

- **Geographically dispersed storage**   You can use iSCSI over existing wide area networks (WANs), whereas Fibre Channel has a practical limit of 10 kilometers.
- **Lower deployment costs**   Fibre Channel requires specialized network infrastructure, while iSCSI can use existing IP network infrastructure.
- **Simplified management**   The Microsoft iSCSI initiator is all you need for implementation and management with an organization's already existing IP network expertise.

- **Enhanced security** iSCSI uses Internet Protocol Security (IPSec) and Challenge Handshake Authentication Protocol (CHAP). Specifically, three levels of security are available with IPSec: Authentication Header (AH), Encapsulating Security Payload (ESP), and AH plus ESP.

Windows Server 2012 introduces a clustered Scale-Out File Server that provides more reliability by replicating file shares for application data. Scale-Out File Server varies from traditional file-server clustering technologies and isn't recommended for scenarios with high-volume operations in which opening, closing, or renaming files occurs frequently.

> **MORE INFO   USING SCALE-OUT FILE SERVER**
>
> See *http://technet.microsoft.com/library/hh831349* for more information on the Scale-Out File Server.

Virtual Fibre Channel

Virtual Fibre Channel is a new feature in Hyper-V that enables virtual client machines to connect directly to Fibre Channel host bus adapters (HBAs).

> **MORE INFO   USING VIRTUAL FIBRE CHANNEL**
>
> See *http://technet.microsoft.com/library/hh831413.aspx* for more information on Virtual Fibre Channel.

Storage Spaces and storage pools

Storage Spaces are a new technology in Windows Server 2012 that uses standard disks in a group. A Storage Space creates a virtualized disk that enables you to combine several disks as needed for redundancy and capacity expansion. Picture Storage Spaces as the software RAID (Redundant Array of Inexpensive Disks) of tomorrow. Storage Spaces have the following features:

- **Resiliency** You can optionally use mirroring or parity to provide for redundancy in case one of the disks fails.

- **Availability** Storage Spaces can use failover clustering, pools can be clustered across nodes, and then the Storage Space is built on top so that if one node fails, another node picks up in its place.

- **Administration** Storage pools and Storage Spaces are integrated with Active Directory and follow a similar model, thus enabling delegation of control.

- **Optimized Capacity** Storage Spaces take advantage of trim storage support to reclaim space. They can share disk across multiple workloads, thus optimizing how disk space is used, thereby reducing waste.

- **Simplified Management** Storage Spaces use the same concepts as storage pools, therefore alleviating administrators from having to learn a new technology. Storage Spaces are also manageable through several interfaces, including Windows PowerShell.

Storage pools and Storage Spaces are created within the File and Storage Services role in Windows Server 2012. The key for planning Storage Spaces is to think of them as virtual disks created from one or more storage pools. Storage Spaces are at the level where the provisioning and resiliency are created, and storage pools are where capacity is expanded.

> ***MORE INFO*** **USING STORAGE SPACES**
>
> See *http://technet.microsoft.com/library/hh831739.aspx* **for more information on Storage Spaces.**

Data deduplication

Data deduplication is another new feature in Windows Server 2012 that helps remove duplicate data to preserve storage capacity. A role service within the File and Storage Services role, data deduplication breaks data into small chunks, identifies the duplicates, and maintains a single copy of each chunk. The following workloads are considered ideal for deduplication:

- **General file shares** house general content, home folders, and offline files.
- **Software deployment shares** house program setup files, images, and the like.
- **VHD libraries** store VHD files for provisioning.

By default, data deduplication doesn't attempt to deduplicate a file until after five days, although this setting can be changed (MinimumFileAgeDays setting). Data deduplication also uses an exclusion list with which you can manually exclude files from deduplication. You can implement data deduplication on non-removable NTFS drives but not on system or boot volumes. Data deduplication runs garbage collection once an hour.

> ***NOTE*** **DATA DEDUPLICATION**
>
> **Data deduplication isn't enabled by default. Also, Cluster Share Volumes (CSVs), system volumes, dynamic disks, and Resilient File System (ReFS) are not eligible for data deduplication. Files smaller than 32KB or those that are encrypted aren't processed.**

After data deduplication is installed, you can use the DDPEVAL.exe command-line tool to estimate capacity savings on Windows 7 or Windows 8 client computers as well as Windows Server 2008 R2 and Windows Server 2012 servers. The Windows PowerShell Measure-DedupFileMetaData cmdlet determines the amount of disk that can be reclaimed by deleting data from a volume.

Configuring the iSCSI Target Server

The goal of configuring an iSCSI Target Server is to make Windows Server 2012 a storage server itself. The iSCSI Target Server role is found within the File and Storage Services role. You also can add the iSCSI Target Server role via Windows PowerShell with this command:

```
Add-WindowsFeature fs-iscsitarget-server
```

After the role is added, you must configure the iSCSI Target Server role through File and Storage Services in Server Manager. Within iSCSI role management, you first need to configure an iSCSI virtual disk, which you can achieve through the New iSCSI Virtual Disk Wizard shown in Figure 1-28.

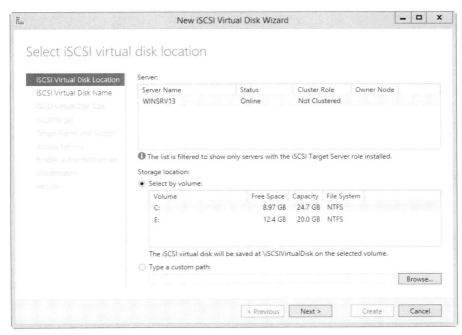

FIGURE 1-28 Configuring an iSCSI virtual disk is a prerequisite to configuring an iSCSI target.

In the New iSCSI Virtual Disk Wizard, you select the disk from a list of volumes on the computer, select its size, and then create a new iSCSI Target, as shown in Figure 1-29.

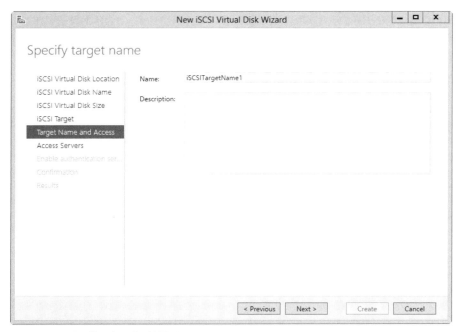

FIGURE 1-29 Configuring the iSCSI Target name.

After the target's name is configured, you select the servers that will act as initiators for the target (see Figure 1-30).

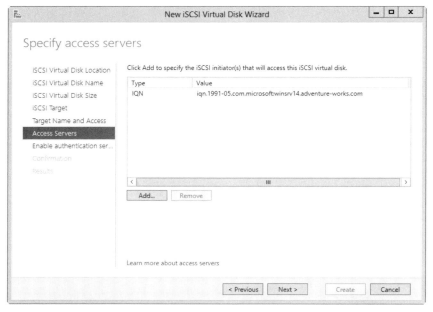

FIGURE 1-30 Configuring the iSCSI initiator.

Clicking Add within that dialog box reveals another dialog box (see Figure 1-31), in which you can select the iSCSI initiator in several different ways.

FIGURE 1-31 Querying for an iSCSI initiator.

As you can see in Figure 1-31, computers prior to Windows Server 2012 don't support the Query capability, which means that you need to add those down-level computers manually by either selecting them (if they've been predefined) or by filling in their IQN or other information.

The final step in the configuration of an iSCSI target is to optionally specify CHAP credentials.

After you complete initial configuration of an iSCSI target, you can change many of its properties through the Properties sheet shown in Figure 1-32.

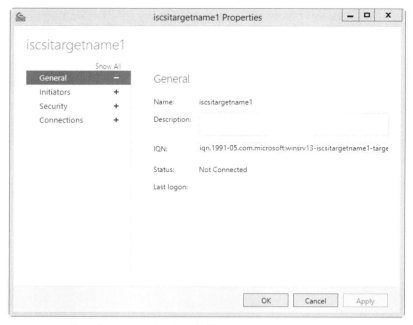

FIGURE 1-32 Changing properties of an iSCSI target.

> **MORE INFO   CONFIGURING ISCSI**
>
> The iSCSI Target Server can also be configured to work in failover cluster mode. This process is configured through Failover Cluster Manager. iSCSI can also work with VDS and VSS. See *http://technet.microsoft.com/library/hh848268.aspx* for more information on configuring iSCSI with these features.

Configuring Internet Storage Name Server

Internet Storage Name Server (iSNS) is a client-server technology that enables discovery, management, and configuration of storage targets such as iSCSI and Fibre Channel. You can add the Microsoft iSNS Server service feature through the Add Roles and Features wizard in Windows Server 2012. Once installed, the service configuration is found within the iSNS Server menu item under the Tools menu.

For iSNS clients to discover the iSCSI targets available, you need to add the iSNS server to the iSCSI Initiator in Windows Server 2012. You do so through the iSCSI Initiator administrative tool, specifically on the Discovery tab shown in Figure 1-33.

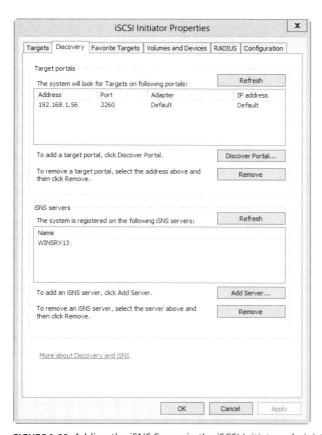

FIGURE 1-33 Adding the iSNS Server in the iSCSI Initiator administrative tool.

After the iSNS Server is added through the iSCSI Initiator, it shows up within the iSNS Server Administrative Tool, as shown in Figure 1-34.

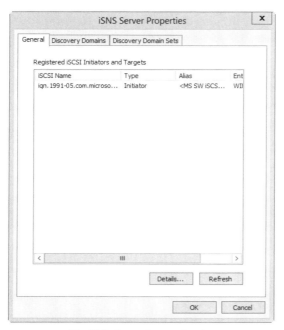

FIGURE 1-34 The iSNS Server Properties sheet.

MORE INFO **ISNS SERVER OVERVIEW**

See *http://technet.microsoft.com/library/cc772568.aspx* for an overview of the iSNS Server.

Configuring Network File System

Network File System (NFS) is a popular means for accessing file resources on UNIX and Linux servers as well as certain virtualization vendors such as VMWare. NFS is a subrole within the File and Storage Services role. Once activated, NFS is managed through the Services for Network File System Administrative Tool. NFS shares are managed through the File and Storage Service management console.

An important component when working with NFS is user identity mapping, which enables users on non-Active Directory systems such as Linux to work with NFS in Windows by enabling NFS clients to loop up external identity information in Active Directory. This process connects the User Identifier (UID) and Group Identifier (GID) from a UNIX environment to a unique Active Directory Security Identifiers (SID) for each user.

This is typically accomplished either through the Identity Management for UNIX or using Active Directory Lightweight Directory Service (AD LDS). Identity Management for UNIX is installed via the Deployment Image Servicing and Management (DISM) tool using these commands:

- Install the administration tools:

  ```
  Dism.exe /online /enable-feature /featurename:adminui /all
  ```

- Install the server for Network Information Service (NIS):

  ```
  Dism.exe /online /enable-feature /featurename:nis /all
  ```

- Install password synchronization:

  ```
  Dism.exe /online /enable-feature /featurename:psync /all
  ```

Mapping via Active Directory Domain Services (AD DS) is the typical enterprise scenario because shares are frequently created to support both SMB and NFS.

MORE INFO **MAPPING WITH AD DS**

See *http://technet.microsoft.com/library/hh509016* for more information on mapping via AD DS.

Mapping via AD LDS is another scenario but less common for enterprises because the method is appropriate for environments that don't already have an existing AD DS infrastructure.

You also can configure the NFS service to allow all connections with no authentication, as discussed later. The authentication options are set when configuring the share and can also be changed later. Figure 1-35 shows the authentication options dialog box for a new share.

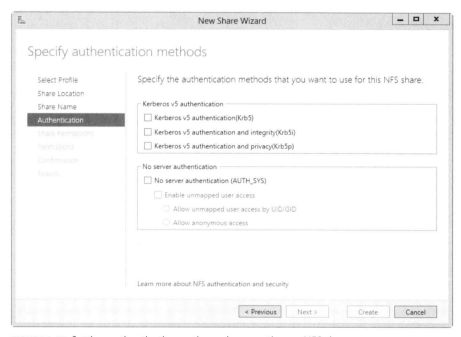

FIGURE 1-35 Setting authentication options when creating an NFS share.

> **NOTE** **ACCOUNT MAPPING**
>
> AD LDS enables account mapping of UNIX UIDs and GIDs to Active Directory accounts; AD DS does not.

Figure 1-36 shows the Authentication pane for a share named E.

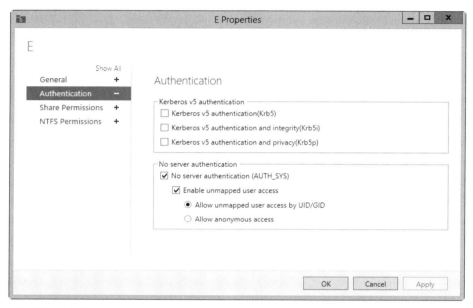

FIGURE 1-36 Authentication properties of an NFS share.

Among the authentication options, Kerberos v5 (Krb5) uses the Kerberos v5 protocol for authentication, Krbv5i provides integrity checking to verify that authentication data has not been altered, and Krb5p provides privacy, which is a new addition for Windows Server 2012.

Unmapped user access is useful for scenarios where integration doesn't occur between the clients accessing the shares. Unmapped user access comes in two forms: anonymous and unmapped. With unmapped, the server for NFS creates custom SIDs that correspond to the UIDs and GIDs for the UNIX accounts accessing the share. When allowing anonymous access, especially root access, your best bet is to use Windows Firewall or other firewalls to deny access to the NFS service from all but the required IP addresses or subnets.

Up to this point only simple file sharing scenarios have been discussed. Using advanced share options for NFS requires that both the NFS Server role and the File Server Resource Manager role be installed. When the File Server Resource Manager is available, you can configure extended properties of NFS shares, including Folder Usage Scenarios and Quotas.

Installing device-specific modules

Storage providers use device-specific modules (DSMs) to extend capabilities of their storage solutions within the Microsoft Multipath I/O (MPIO) framework. For example, storage providers might use a DSM to provide additional high availability or clustering capabilities with their storage solutions. DSMs are also provided.

Because DSMs are part of MPIO, they're installed through the Multipath I/O feature (added as a Feature through the Add Roles and Features Wizard). Using the vendor's DSM setup tool to install DSMs is recommended. However, you also can install DSMs through the INF file provided by the storage provider. In this case, installation is accomplished through the MPIO Administrative Tool on the DSM Install tab, shown in Figure 1-37.

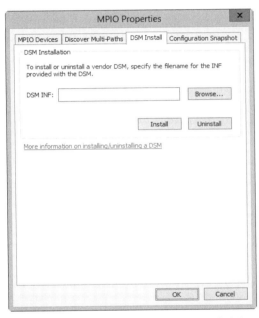

FIGURE 1-37 Installing a DSM in the MPIO Administrative Tool.

> **NOTE COMPLIANCE**
>
> DSMs provided by third-party storage providers must be SPC-3 compliant.

THOUGHT EXPERIMENT
Configuring NFS

In the following thought experiment, apply what you've learned about this objective. You can find answers to these questions in the "Answers" section at the end of this chapter.

You need to configure NFS in your environment. The NFS server handles important shares for Linux-based servers. The Linux servers provide a mount point using NFS but otherwise won't authenticate at the user level.

1. Identify the steps and/or settings necessary for this NFS server configuration.

2. What additional steps can be taken to enhance security in this environment?

Objective summary

- Windows Server 2012 introduces numerous enhancements around the File and Storage Services role. Specific among these are Storage Spaces, the iSCSI target server, trim storage, and data deduplication.
- Storage Spaces allow for more flexibility in the use of storage pools.
- Trim storage and data deduplication help optimize capacity by reducing repeated data and reclaiming under-utilized storage.
- The iSNS Name Server service enables client discover of iSCSI and Fibre Channel storage.
- Windows Server 2012 enhances Network File Server (NFS) support by extending the authentication methods available.
- Device-Specific Modules (DSMs) relate to Multipath I/O for Fibre Channel connections. You manage this feature through the MPIO Properties sheet.

Objective review

Answer the following questions to test your knowledge of the information in this objective. You can find the answers to these questions and explanations of why each answer choice is correct or incorrect in the "Answers" section at the end of this chapter.

1. Which command adds the iSCSI Target Server role to Windows Server 2012?

    A. Add-WindowsFeature fs-iscsi-server

    B. Add-WindowsFeature fs-iscsitarget-server

    C. Add-WindowsFeature iscsitarget-server

    D. Add-WindowsFeature fs-iscsitarget

2. Which of the following are not eligible for data deduplication?

   A. CSV

   B. ReFS

   C. NTFS

   D. ext3

3. What is the default file age for data deduplication?

   A. 7 days

   B. 3 days

   C. 30 days

   D. 5 days

4. iSCSI requires that which two roles or services be available?

   A. iSCSI Initiator and Storage Spaces

   B. iSCSI Target and iSNS Initiator

   C. iSCSI Target and iSCSI Initiator

   D. iSNS Server and iSCSI Target Server

Chapter summary

- Designing an automated server deployment strategy involves several Microsoft tools, including the Windows Assessment and Deployment Kit (ADK) and Windows Deployment Services (WDS).
- WDS is central to a server deployment strategy.
- Server migration typically involves upgrading from one version to another.
- Virtual Machine Manager configures complex virtualized infrastructures.
- Storage Spaces is an important feature for maximizing use of raw storage.

Answers

This section contains the solutions to the thought experiments and answers to the objective review questions in this chapter.

Objective 1.1: Thought experiment

1. The basic steps include creating a capture image from a reference computer, and then prestaging the clients from within the WDS server manager. When prestaging the client, you can choose the image to be used for deployment.

2. The basic steps involve making sure that the server can be reached from the network segment from which the WDS server is deployed and making sure that the WDS server is first to respond to the PXE request.

Objective 1.1: Review

1. **Correct Answer:** B

   A. **Incorrect:** A Preinstallation image isn't used to capture an image from a computer.

   B. **Correct:** A Capture image is used to capture an image from a computer.

   C. **Incorrect:** A Discover image isn't used to capture an image from a computer.

   D. **Incorrect:** A Virtualization image isn't a real type of image as defined by Microsoft.

2. **Correct Answer:** C

   A. **Incorrect:** This isn't a valid command.

   B. **Incorrect:** This isn't a valid command.

   C. **Correct:** The command wdsutil /set-server /resetbootprogram:yes resets the boot so that you don't need to press F12 on reboot.

   D. **Incorrect:** This isn't a valid command.

3. **Correct Answer:** A

   A. **Correct:** DISM is used to mount images.

   B. **Incorrect:** WDS isn't used to mount images for servicing.

   C. **Incorrect:** Windows Image Administration isn't used for this purpose.

   D. **Incorrect:** Advanced Image Kit (AIK) isn't used to mount images for servicing.

4. **Correct Answer:** B

   A. **Incorrect:** Option 31 isn't used for this purpose.

   B. **Correct:** Option 60 is used to inform DHCP clients of the WDS server.

C. Incorrect: Boot Option 4 isn't a real option.

D. Incorrect: WDS Server Option isn't a real option.

Objective 1.2: Thought experiment

1. The servers should share an image store that would likely be configured using File Replication Services (FRS).

2. The PXE responses must match between the servers and should be configured so that the clients obtain the image and reboot to the image.

3. You should create client unattended files and use the Add Prestaged Client Wizard, as shown in this objective.

Objective 1.2: Review

1. **Correct Answers:** A and C

   A. Correct: Deployment is one available mode for the WDS server.

   B. Incorrect: Image Response isn't a valid option.

   C. Correct: Transport is a valid mode of operation for WDS.

   D. Incorrect: Capture isn't a valid mode of operation for WDS.

2. **Correct Answer:** B

   A. Incorrect: Configuring boot order so that the correct deployment server is chosen isn't a valid option.

   B. Correct: Prestaging the client within WDS on the correct server ensures that the correct server responds to the request.

   C. Incorrect: Configuring the correct image for the location chosen isn't valid.

   D. Incorrect: Using multicast to ensure the most effective use of bandwidth isn't relevant to this solution.

3. **Correct Answer:** A

   A. Correct: At a future time and/or when a threshold of clients request an image is the correct answer.

   B. Incorrect: At a future time and/or when the server comes online isn't a valid combination. You can schedule for a future time, but it's assumed that the server is online and in any event it's not a configurable option.

   C. Incorrect: Immediately or at a scheduled time isn't valid. You can schedule for a future time, but immediately isn't a direct option.

   D. Incorrect: When the client threshold is met or daily isn't valid. You can set a threshold but not a daily schedule.

Objective 1.3: Thought experiment

1. Network Load Balancing is appropriate for this solution because HTTP is a stateless protocol.

2. Virtualization Host Backup is likely the most appropriate here, but as long as both machines are online, the other backup methods could be appropriate, assuming that one machine is taken offline during its backup so as to not negatively affect response time.

Objective 1.3: Review

1. **Correct Answer:** D

    A. **Incorrect:** Determine the Virtualization Scope is one of the planning steps.

    B. **Incorrect:** Summarize and Analyze Workload Requirements is one of the planning steps.

    C. **Incorrect:** Create a List of Workloads is one of the planning steps.

    D. **Correct:** Optimize Workload Resources isn't one of the steps in planning server virtualization.

2. **Correct Answer:** A

    A. **Correct:** An External trust is a trust between domains in different forests.

    B. **Incorrect:** This type of trust doesn't exist.

    C. **Incorrect:** This type of trust doesn't exist.

    D. **Incorrect:** This type of trust doesn't exist.

3. **Correct Answer:** B

    A. **Incorrect:** This command doesn't exist.

    B. **Correct:** Use the Add-PSSnapin Microsoft.Windows.ServerManager.Migration command to add the Windows Server Migration Tools.

    C. **Incorrect:** This command doesn't exist.

    D. **Incorrect:** This command doesn't exist.

4. **Correct Answer:** D

    A. **Incorrect:** SSH isn't used for this communication.

    B. **Incorrect:** Remote API isn't a valid communication option.

    C. **Incorrect:** SMB isn't used for this communication.

    D. **Correct:** WMI is used for this communication.

5. **Correct Answer:** D

  A. **Incorrect:** This isn't the recommendation.

  B. **Incorrect:** This isn't the recommendation.

  C. **Incorrect:** This isn't the recommendation.

  D. **Correct:** Seven days of data collection is recommended.

Objective 1.4: Thought experiment

1. Open the service template and create a copy of it so that a new service template can be created.

2. Add the ability to scale the tier out in the Service Template Designer.

Objective 1.4: Review

1. **Correct Answer:** A

  A. **Correct:** Service Template Designer is used to edit or change service templates.

  B. **Incorrect:** Virtual Service Editor isn't a real tool in VMM.

  C. **Incorrect:** Service Resource Library isn't used for this purpose.

  D. **Incorrect:** Virtual Template Designer isn't a real tool in VMM.

2. **Correct Answer:** C

  A. **Incorrect:** Logical networks are not managed in the Resources workspace.

  B. **Incorrect:** Logical networks are not managed in the Library workspace.

  C. **Correct:** Logical networks are managed in the Fabric workspace.

  D. **Incorrect:** Logical networks are not managed in the Network Services workspace.

3. **Correct Answer:** A

  A. **Correct:** A Capability profile is used to determine whether a machine is deployed in a highly available manner.

  B. **Incorrect:** A Hardware profile isn't used for this purpose.

  C. **Incorrect:** This profile isn't used to determine whether a machine is deployed in a highly available manner.

  D. **Incorrect:** This profile isn't used to determine whether a machine is deployed in a highly available manner.

Objective 1.5: Thought experiment

1. In the Authentication section for the share in the NFS management console, select the option to allow unmapped user access as well as anonymous access.

2. Firewalling should be implemented to ensure that only the Linux servers can connect to the NFS ports on the Windows server housing the NFS service.

Objective 1.5: Review

1. **Correct Answer:** B

   A. **Incorrect:** This isn't the correct option for the command.

   B. **Correct:** Add-WindowsFeature fs-iscsitarget-server is the correct command and option.

   C. **Incorrect:** This isn't the correct option for the command.

   D. **Incorrect:** This isn't the correct option for the command.

2. **Correct Answers:** A, B, and D

   A. **Correct:** CSV isn't eligible for data deduplication.

   B. **Correct:** ReFS isn't eligible for data deduplication.

   C. **Incorrect:** NTFS is eligible for data deduplication.

   D. **Correct:** ext3 isn't eligible for data deduplication.

3. **Correct Answer:** D

   A. **Incorrect:** This isn't the correct age for deduplication.

   B. **Incorrect:** This isn't the correct age for deduplication.

   C. **Incorrect:** This isn't the correct age for deduplication.

   D. **Correct:** Five days is the default data deduplication age.

4. **Correct Answer:** C

   A. **Incorrect:** Storage Spaces aren't relevant to iSCSI.

   B. **Incorrect:** There is no iSNS Initiator service.

   C. **Correct:** iSCSI requires both an iSCSI target and an iSCSI initiator.

   D. **Incorrect:** An iSNS server isn't required for iSCSI.

CHAPTER 2

Design and implement network infrastructure services

A network infrastructure consists of those basic services like Dynamic Host Configuration Protocol (DHCP), Domain Name System (DNS), and Internet Protocol (IP) address management. Windows Server 2012 provides all these services. New to Windows Server 2012 is a service called IPAM, short for IP address management. IPAM gives an organization a single location from which the addressing for the entire organization can be managed and monitored.

Objectives in this chapter:

- Objective 2.1: Design and maintain a Dynamic Host Configuration Protocol (DHCP) solution
- Objective 2.2: Design a name resolution solution strategy
- Objective 2.3: Design and manage an IP address management solution

Objective 2.1: Design and maintain a Dynamic Host Configuration Protocol (DHCP) solution

Dynamic Host Configuration Protocol (DHCP) supplies Internet Protocol (IP) addresses and other network configuration information to devices on a network. Most clients and client devices in an enterprise use DHCP to obtain network information.

This objective covers the following topics:

- Design considerations, including a highly available DHCP solution that includes split scope, DHCP failover, DHCP failover clustering, DHCP interoperability, and DHCPv6
- How to implement DHCP filtering
- How to implement and configure a DHCP management pack
- How to maintain a DHCP database

Designing a highly available DHCP solution

DHCP is a vital service on an enterprise network. Without it, clients can't obtain IP addresses and information such as DNS servers. For this reason, DHCP is frequently deployed in a highly available manner so that if one server becomes unavailable, another can take over. This section examines the considerations involved in designing a high availability solution for DHCP.

> **MORE INFO**   **TERMINOLOGY AND BASIC DHCP DESIGN**
>
> This section concentrates on DHCP design at the enterprise level and assumes that you have requisite knowledge of DHCP itself, along with basic deployment and management of DHCP. See *http://technet.microsoft.com/library/dd283016* for more information on DHCP, including terminology and basic design.

The two goals for highly available DHCP are as follows:

- Provide DHCP service at all times.
- When one DHCP server is no longer available, enable clients to extend their lease by contacting a different DHCP server.

When designing a highly available DHCP solution, you should consider whether to provide split-scope DHCP or failover clustering.

Split scope

With split-scope DHCP, two servers provide address and network information using a portion of the address space or DHCP scope. For example, if an organization assigns addresses from the 192.168.100.0/24 subnet, a split-scope DHCP scenario might call for 80 percent of the addresses to be assigned by one server and the other 20 percent by another server. This is known as the "80/20" rule for DHCP scope assignment, and organizations sometimes place the server with 80 percent of the scope nearest to the clients. However, you don't need to figure out the 80/20 split; the Dhcp Split-Scope Configuration Wizard includes a step to help configure the split (see Figure 2-1).

FIGURE 2-1 Configuring a split-scope percentage in the Dhcp Split-Scope Configuration Wizard.

Split scope enables traffic to be split among participating servers while also providing redundancy for clients should one of the two servers fail. However, clients accept the first DHCP response they receive, so you can't guarantee from which server clients will receive a DHCP response. If the servers are split across a network boundary, you need to configure a DHCP relay agent on a router and introduce a delay at that point so as to prevent the secondary server from responding before the primary server. The Dhcp Split-Scope Configuration Wizard also includes an opportunity to add a delay to one of the servers involved in the split scope, as shown in Figure 2-2.

FIGURE 2-2 Adding a delay in a split scope can help ensure that network information comes from the correct server.

Alternatively, a delay can be configured into the scope itself through the Advanced tab in the Scope Properties sheet, as shown in Figure 2-3.

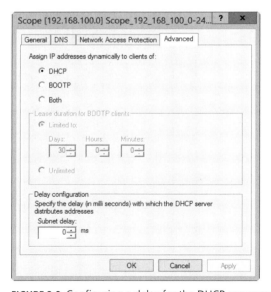

FIGURE 2-3 Configuring a delay for the DHCP server response can help in a split-scope scenario.

DHCP failover

A new feature of Windows Server 2012, DHCP failover means that two servers are configured with the same DHCP configuration. Windows Server 2012 has two modes for failover: hot standby and load sharing. These modes of DHCP failover are different from failover clustering, which is discussed later.

With DHCP failover, each server has a replicated version of the entire scope, including lease information. This means that either server can offer addresses for the entire scope. The practical implication of scope and lease replication is to enable both modes of operation. With a hot standby operation, one server provides DHCP information while the other server maintains a replicated version of the DHCP lease information, ready to take over if the primary server fails. In a load-sharing mode, each server assigns DHCP information and updates the shared lease information database.

Hot standby mode is useful for organizations that have a remote location with DHCP clients, sometimes called a hub-and-spoke topology. The remote location acts as the primary server; a server at the central data center acts as a backup. If the remote server goes offline, the secondary server at the data center can take over. The primary and secondary assignment is done at the subnet level, rather than the scope level. This means that a server can be primary for one subnet and secondary for another subnet.

Load-sharing mode is helpful for data center or centralized DHCP scenarios in which two servers operate within a single site. In load-sharing mode, each server assigns DHCP information to clients based on a load ratio. You set the load balance percentage at configuration time, as shown in Figure 2-4.

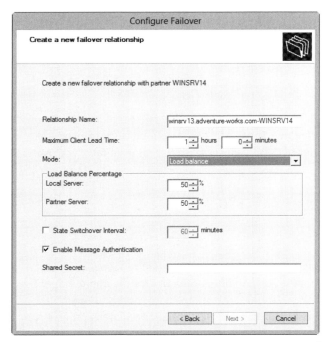

FIGURE 2-4 Configuring the load balance percentage in a DHCP failover architecture.

You can edit the load balance percentage after initial configuration from the partner server.

DHCP failover clustering

A redundant architecture available prior to Windows Server 2012 is failover clustering. With failover clustering, the primary DHCP server offers DHCP information, and the secondary server takes over if the first server fails. In this scenario, the DHCP servers share the same storage, thus making a single point of failure at the storage level.

DHCP Interoperability

The term *interoperability* refers to the relationship between DHCP and other Microsoft technologies such as Routing and Remote Access, Network Access Protection (NAP), Active Directory Domain Services (AD DS), and other related technologies, rather than interoperability between the Microsoft DHCP implementation and the DHCP implementation from other vendors.

DHCP clients can register dynamic DNS entries upon address assignment. To do so, the DHCP server depends on a directory services domain controller to be available, and the DHCP server must be authorized to make such entries into the DNS. This can be configured on the DNS tab of the Scope Properties sheet (see Figure 2-5).

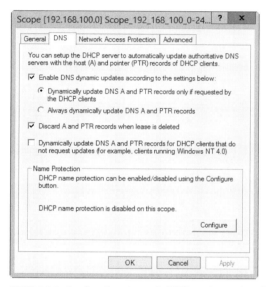

FIGURE 2-5 Configuring dynamic DNS settings related to a DHCP scope.

The DHCP server can update both the pointer (PTR) and host address (A) record for the client. The Client FQDN option (DHCP option 81) is used for this purpose. Option 81 includes the Fully Qualified Domain Name (FQDN) and other information from the client. As Figure 2-5 shows, the server can be configured to update the DNS at all times or only if requested by the client. Older clients are also supported (ones that can't or don't send DHCP option 81) by selecting the Dynamically Update DNS A And PTR Records For DHCP Clients That Do Not Request Updates check box within this Properties sheet.

DHCP interoperability with AD DS is typically used to detect and authorize additional DHCP servers on the network. DHCP servers running Windows can be authorized into the AD DS schema and if not authorized, can be prevented from leasing IP addresses to clients. However, this authorization scheme works only for DHCP servers running Windows 2000 and above and doesn't work for a DHCP server running on Linux or a network device.

DHCP can work with NAP to limit client access unless the client is in a compliant state. Figure 2-6 shows the NAP-related configuration in a scope's Properties sheet.

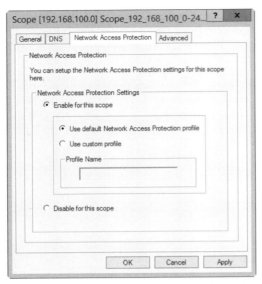

FIGURE 2-6 Network Access Protection settings related to DHCP.

You can configure NAP at the individual scope level or for all scopes on a server.

> **MORE INFO WORKING WITH NAP**
>
> For more information on NAP, see *http://technet.microsoft.com/library/dd125338%28*.

DHCPv6 considerations

DHCP for IPv6 operates in stateless and stateful modes. In stateful mode, clients obtain both an address and information such as DNS servers from the DHCP server. In stateless mode, clients obtain ancillary information such as DNS servers but receive their addressing through IPv6 auto-configuration or as a static IP address.

Implementing DHCP filtering

DHCP filtering, sometimes called *link-layer filtering*, enables you to configure how the DHCP server responds to requests for address and network information. DHCP filtering enables the DHCP server to send information only to known clients or deny information to specific clients. This is especially important in a data-center scenario in which you likely want to control the devices allowed on the network.

DHCP filtering works with Media Access Control (MAC) addresses, which are sent by the DHCP client along with a DHCP request. Windows Server 2012 has two types of filters: Allow and Deny. An Allow filter sends network information only to those clients listed in the filter. A Deny filter excludes specific clients from obtaining information from the DHCP server.

In an Allow scenario, each authorized MAC address needs to be specifically entered into the filter; otherwise, it can't obtain information from the DHCP server. Of course, this isn't an issue if the client is using an address that's statically assigned on the client itself.

Windows Server 2012 enables filtering with the full MAC address or by using wildcards. For example, these are all valid filters:

- 00-11-09-7c-ef-57
- 00-11-09-7c-ef-*
- 00-11-09-*-*-*
- 0011097cef57

Using wildcards enables you to configure a group of the same devices or devices from the same manufacturer as being allowed or denied. This saves the effort of entering each MAC address individually if a group of devices share the same MAC prefix.

DHCP filtering is configured with the DHCP MMC snap-in. Adding a filtered address is accomplished by right-clicking either Allow or Deny (depending on which type you want to set up) and then entering the MAC address details, as shown in Figure 2-7.

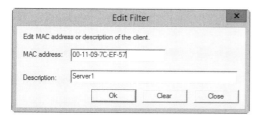

FIGURE 2-7 Creating a DHCP filter.

You also need to enable filters at the overall filter (Allow or Deny) level rather than at the individual MAC address level. To enable the Allow or Deny filter, right-click Allow or Deny in the DHCP MMC snap-in and select Enable. You can also enable filters at the scope level.

Implementing and configuring a DHCP Management Pack

The DHCP Management Pack, part of the Operations Manager component of Microsoft System Center 2012, enables advanced logging and monitoring of the DHCP environment. For example, the DHCP Management Pack enables monitoring of the availability of the DHCP service, the filtering status, and the status of scopes to help prevent scope exhaustion.

Implementing a DHCP Management Pack requires Microsoft System Center 2012. The DHCP Management Pack is imported into Operations Manager. Creating a new management pack is recommended to incorporate any changes to the DHCP Management Pack without affecting the original configuration.

Table 2-1 outlines several scenarios for monitoring a DHCP infrastructure.

TABLE 2-1 Common scenarios for DHCP monitoring

What to Monitor	Description
The servers themselves	Monitor for the availability of the service and detect unauthorized DHCP servers.
DHCP scopes	Monitor when a scope is nearing address exhaustion.
The DHCP database	Monitor when the database is having problems.
Performance	Monitor for excessive requests or queue length as well as the number of addresses in use, and related items.

MORE INFO **DHCP MANAGEMENT PACK**

See *http://technet.microsoft.com/library/cc180306.aspx* **for more information on the DHCP Management Pack**

Maintaining a DHCP database

Maintenance of a DHCP database involves backing up and restoring the database. The location of the database and its backup location can be configured at the server level within its Properties sheet, as shown in Figure 2-8.

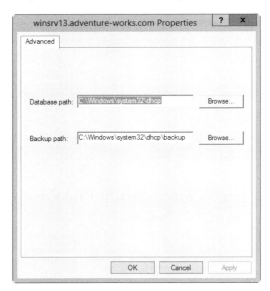

FIGURE 2-8 Configuring the location of the DHCP database, as well as its backup location.

You can back up and restore the DHCP database through Actions at the server level in DHCP Manager. Also, to change an automated backup that runs every 60 minutes, set the

BackupInterval value in the registry at HKEY_LOCAL_MACHINE\SYSTEM\CurrentControlSet\Services\DHCPServer\Parameters.

> ***MORE INFO*** **COMPACTING WITH JETPACK**
>
> **You also can compact the DHCP database by using Jetpack. See *http://technet.microsoft.com/library/hh875589%28v=ws.10%29.aspx* for more information.**

At times you may need to reconcile the database due to inconsistencies in client addressing between summary and detailed information. To do so, select Reconcile All Scopes from the address level (IPv4 or IPv6) or at the scope level by clicking Reconcile.

THOUGHT EXPERIMENT
Designing a DHCP topology

In the following thought experiment, apply what you've learned about this objective. You can find answers to these questions in the "Answers" section at the end of this chapter.

You have a wide area network (WAN)–connected remote site with 150 clients that need to receive address information and a primary data center that provides DHCP information for 350 clients.

Describe the DHCP topology that should be designed for this site, including hot standby and failover architecture, if applicable.

Objective summary

- The DHCP server role in Windows Server 2012 provides for redundancy with split scope, failover through hot standby and load sharing, and failover clustering.
- Hot standby failover enables a server to take over should its counterpart fail.
- Load-sharing failover enables both servers to assign DHCP information.
- Failover clustering enables both servers to assign DHCP information by sharing the same DHCP database on a shared storage location.
- DHCP filtering configures how the server responds to clients by using link-layer MAC addresses.
- The DHCP Management Pack, part of System Center Operations Manager, enables monitoring and reporting of the DHCP service.
- The DHCP database is stored on the file system and needs to be reconciled occasionally to remove stale entries.

Objective review

Answer the following questions to test your knowledge of the information in this objective. You can find the answers to these questions and explanations of why each answer choice is correct or incorrect in the "Answers" section at the end of this chapter.

1. You're configuring a split-scope DHCP scenario between two servers. What's the recommended percentage for a DHCP split scope configuration?

   A. 60/40

   B. 70/30

   C. 80/20

   D. 50/50

2. Which of the following are valid MAC filters in Windows Server 2012? (You can assume that the MAC addresses themselves are valid.)

   A. 00-11-09-*-*-*

   B. 001109001111

   C. 00:11:09:09:11:09

   D. 00-11-09-7c-ef-%

3. You need to move the DHCP database. Assuming a standard Windows directory and Program Files path structure and that you've changed the path in the DHCP Manager, what's the default path where the DHCP database is found?

   A. C:\Windows\system32\dhcp

   B. C:\Program Files\Microsoft\DHCP\Data

   C. C:\Windows\system32\DHCP\Data

   D. HKEY_LOCAL_MACHINE\SOFTWARE\Microsoft\DHCP

4. While implementing split scope, you notice that the secondary server is responding to numerous DHCP requests first. What's the best way to handle this situation?

   A. Increase the split ratio so that the secondary server has more IP addresses from the scope.

   B. Introduce a delay for DHCP offers from the secondary using the DHCP management console.

   C. Reduce the load on the primary server so that it can respond faster.

   D. Place the secondary DHCP server on a different network segment to introduce a delay in the response.

Objective 2.2: Design a name resolution solution strategy

Name resolution typically involves Domain Name System (DNS) but can also include Windows Internet Name Service (WINS). This objective concentrates on design of the solution rather than its implementation.

This objective covers just this topic:

- Design considerations, including secure name resolution, DNSSEC, DNS socket pool, cache locking, disjoint namespaces, DNS interoperability, migration to application partitions, IPv6, Single-Label DNS Name Resolution, zone hierarchy, and zone delegation

Designing a name resolution strategy

You need to keep several things in mind when designing a complex name resolution strategy at the enterprise level. These include prioritizing security while at the same time providing a reliable and robust infrastructure for the organization. Several features of Windows Server 2012 can be used to create this robust and reliable design.

In addition to the features you can use to create a robust and reliable design, you should also be intimately familiar with DNS for the exam. This includes being familiar with the DNS protocol as well as the tools and concepts surrounding implementation of DNS in an enterprise. Many of these tools and concepts have existed for quite some time and aren't directly called out as objectives on the exam. As an enterprise administrator, you are expected to have the prerequisite knowledge of a primary protocol such as DNS.

> **MORE INFO**   **ADDITIONAL REFERENCES**
>
> Table 2-2 provides links to additional reference information for these concepts, but you're encouraged to pursue supplemental DNS information beyond that which is listed here and on the exam objectives.

TABLE 2-2 Additional resources

Concept	More Information
Conditional forwarding	*http://technet.microsoft.com/library/0104be3c-0405-4455-b011-6950875c0446*
DNS zone types	*http://technet.microsoft.com/library/cc771898*
DNS server placement	*http://technet.microsoft.com/library/cc737361*
Troubleshooting DNS	*http://technet.microsoft.com/library/cc753041*
DNS Technical Reference	*http://technet.microsoft.com/library/dd197461*

Secure name resolution

Ensuring secure name resolution includes making sure that the name server and DNS server have been secured. The Advanced tab in the DNS server Properties sheet, shown in Figure 2-9, contains several check boxes relevant to secure name resolution.

FIGURE 2-9 Advanced DNS properties for the DNS Server service.

Among the options relevant to DNS security is Secure Cache Against Pollution, which randomizes the source port for requests, and Enable DNSSEC Validation For Remote Responses, which is discussed in the "DNSSEC" section later in this chapter.

Several other design considerations should be examined when looking at the name resolution strategy. If clients will resolve external DNS names, such as for Internet hosts, you can configure a group of DNS servers in the forest root domain to forward queries to external DNS servers or by using root hints so that any child domain servers forward queries to the forest root domain servers.

This is essentially what you'll do by disabling recursion on a child DNS server. You can disable recursion for DNS servers that are authoritative for DNS zones but don't need to provide general DNS resolution to clients on the network. A good example of this is an enterprise scenario in which the domain controllers are separate from the DNS servers that clients use for normal Internet name resolution. In such a scenario, recursion should be disabled on the domain controllers. If your domain has both types of records, you should consider splitting the DNS namespace between external and internal servers.

Zone transfers should be disabled by default and enabled only to allowed hosts.

DNSSEC

DNSSEC, defined primarily by RFCs 4033, 4034, and 4035, adds security to DNS. Windows Server 2012 enhances support for DNSSEC (DNS Security Extensions). DNSSEC provides new resource records and also provides for data integrity, origin authority, and authenticated denial of existence. DNSSEC operates using public key cryptography whereby clients receive cryptographically signed responses to queries. The clients have the public key of the server signing the response and can therefore ensure the validity of the response, and that it hasn't been tampered with.

DNSSEC can also sign entire zones via the dnscmd.exe tool. With Windows Server 2012, you can now deploy DNSSEC in Active Directory–integrated zones with dynamic updates. This is a change from previous versions of Windows and its support for DNSSEC.

DNSSEC establishes a chain of trust with a trust anchor at the root zone that enables a chain of trust to be built to ensure that responses are trustworthy. Therefore, when planning to use DNSSEC, you need to determine the location for the trust anchors. This also means that the validity of not only individual resource records can be verified, but also the actual server itself can be verified as being the correct authoritative server.

A signed zone contains RRSIG, DNSKEY, and NSEC records in addition to the normal DNS records in that zone. NSEC provides authenticated denial of existence for DNS. Windows Server 2012 supports NSEC and NSEC3, an extended version of the standard. NSEC3 helps to prevent zone enumeration whereby an attacker can send repeated queries across a zone to determine targets.

> **MORE INFO**   **DEPLOYING DNSSEC**
>
> For a step-by-step demonstration for deploying DNSSEC, visit *http://technet.microsoft .com/library/hh831411*.

DNS socket pool

The DNS socket pool enables randomization of queries to prevent cache poisoning attacks. Security update MS08-037 enables this feature by default, and it is enabled by default in Windows Server 2012. The DNS socket pool uses several source ports for issuing queries.

Both the number of source ports to be used and any exclusions or ports not to be used for issuing queries can be configured. Unfortunately, this feature can't be controlled using the DNS management tool and must instead be configured by using either the dnscmd tool or the registry.

> **MORE INFO** **CONFIGURING THE DNS SOCKET POOL**
>
> See *http://technet.microsoft.com/library/ee649174.aspx* for more information on configuring the socket pool.

Cache locking

Another method for preventing cache poisoning is with cache locking. Cache locking prevents cached responses from being overwritten during their Time to Live (TTL). Cache locking is configured as a percentage of the TTL. So if the TTL is 3600 seconds, a cache-locking percentage of 50 would prevent the cached value from being overwritten for 1800 seconds, or 50 percent of the TTL. You can configure cache locking by using the CacheLockingPercent registry key or the dmscmd tool.

> **MORE INFO** **CONFIGURING CACHE LOCKING**
>
> See *http://technet.microsoft.com/library/ee649148.aspx* for more information on configuring cache locking.

Disjoint namespaces

A disjoint namespace has a different Active Directory domain and DNS domain suffix. For example, a DNS suffix of corp.adventure-works.com with an Active Directory domain of int.corp.adventure-works.com is in a disjoint namespace. Domain members register resource records in the domain in which they're members—int.corp.adventure-works.com in the example. The domain controller then registers both global and site-specific service (SRV) records into the DNS domain. The SRV records are also placed in the _msdcs zone.

Disjoint namespaces are used when business rules dictate that namespace separation needs to occur. However, applications to be used in a disjoint namespace should be tested because they may expect that the domain and DNS suffix match and therefore may not work. Disjoint namespaces require additional administration overhead because of the manual processes involved to manage the DNS and Active Directory information.

The following configurations support disjoint namespaces:

- In a multi-domain Active Directory forest with a single DNS namespace or zone
- In a single Active Directory domain that's split into multiple DNS zones

On the other hand, a disjoint namespace won't work in the following configurations:

- When a suffix matches an Active Directory domain in the current or another forest
- When a certification authority (CA) domain member changes its DNS suffix

DNS interoperability

Microsoft's implementation of DNS complies with the relevant DNS-related RFCs, thus making interoperability possible with other servers. The Enable BIND Secondaries check box on the Advanced tab of the DNS server Properties sheet enables the Windows-based DNS server to interact with a server running the BIND name server. Refer to Figure 2-9 for a screenshot of this tab.

Migration to application partitions

Application partitions enable certain data to be replicated along partition lines. Specifically, application partitions assist with control of the replication's scope—for instance, to enable certain DNS zones to be replicated.

An application partition is created with the dnscmd command-line tool:

```
dnscmd <ServerName> /CreateDirectoryPartition <Fully Qualified Domain Name>
```

After the partition is created, servers are enlisted with this command:

```
dnscmd <ServerName> /EnlistDirectoryPartition <Fully Qualified Domain Name>
```

After the directory partition is created, you can change zone replication in the Properties sheet for the given zone. On the General tab of the zone's Properties sheet, you change the replication configuration by clicking Change. Figure 2-10 shows the General tab.

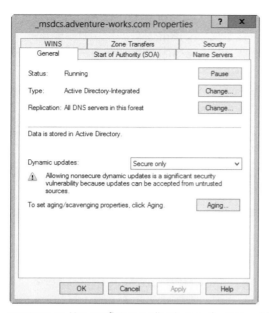

FIGURE 2-10 You configure replication on the General tab of a zone's Properties sheet.

When you click Change, the Change Zone Replication Scope dialog box appears, as in Figure 2-11.

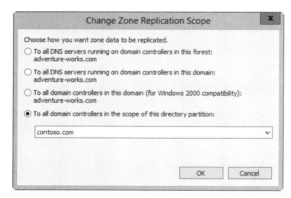

FIGURE 2-11 Replicating to a directory partition.

IPv6

Windows Server 2012 supports IPv6 DNS hosting. Address records are known as AAAA in IPv6 rather than the A record for IPv6 DNS hosts. Designing IPv6 DNS typically means a coexistence strategy of some nature whereby both IPv4 and IPv6 DNS is supported on a network.

MORE INFO **USING IPV6 IN WINDOWS**

See *http://technet.microsoft.com/network/bb530961.aspx* for more information on IPv6 in Windows.

Windows Internet Name Service (WINS) doesn't support IPv6, so keep this limitation in mind when planning an IPv6 deployment. You can use an ISATAP router to provide translation services for WINS.

MORE INFO **USING ISATAP**

See *http://technet.microsoft.com/library/dd379548%28.aspx* for more information on using ISATAP for this purpose.

Single-label DNS name resolution

Single-label domains are missing a top-level domain (TLD) and the normal dot (.) notation associated with domain names. For example, a normal domain is adventure-works.com, whereas a single-label domain is adventure-works.

You find single-label names on networks with legacy Windows Internet Name Service (WINS) deployments. However, as WINS is retired, administrators must plan for providing name resolution for older, legacy WINS-based applications and important resources. Windows has a GlobalNames Zone (GNZ) that can be used to provide name resolution for single-label names. GNZ can be deployed in a single forest or across multiple forests to provide static name resolution.

GNZ helps in the transition from WINS to the multi-label standard DNS zones and can therefore be part of a planning strategy for name resolution. You should understand how GNZ varies from domain suffixes and how it has improved performance over multiple domain suffixes in single-label resolution scenarios with several domains. Windows Server 2012 looks first in the GNZ when a single-label resolution query is received. If a record is in the GNZ, it can't participate in dynamic updates, and dynamic update requests for that record will be refused.

MORE INFO **WORKING WITH THE GNZ**

See *http://technet.microsoft.com/library/cc794961.aspx* for more information, including the exact steps required to configure a GlobalNames Zone. See also *http://technet.microsoft.com/en-us/library/cc816610* for a discussion around the ways in which GNZ can help with resolution.

Zone hierarchy and zone delegation

The zone hierarchy is the tree-like structure of DNS, in which the root of the zone is represented by a single dot (.). Up the tree from that root are top-level domains (TLDs) such as .com, .net, and .org. The tree branches out into the private domains that you recognize, like microsoft.com and adventure-works.com.

Zone delegation refers to the ability to respond to queries authoritatively by using a portion of a zone. For example, in the hierarchical nature of DNS, the root servers are responsible for the root of the zone and delegate authority for TLDs to TLD servers who then delegate responsibility for domains such as adventure-works.com to private corporate nameservers. When a query arrives for www.adventure-works.com, the query begins at the root server, which refers the query to the responsible server for the .com TLD, which then refers to the responsible server for the domain being queried.

In much the same way that root servers delegate to TLD servers, which then delegate to corporate nameservers, you can also delegate portions of corporate domains such as adventure-works.com to other nameservers so that they become authoritative for that part of the zone. For example, you may want to create an authoritative zone for corp.adventure-works.com so that queries are sent to a different server for hosts in that domain.

Zone delegation is configured in the DNS Manager by right-clicking the zone to be delegated and then selecting New Delegation. Doing so invokes the New Zone Delegation Wizard so that the portion of the zone, such as the corp subdomain in the corp.adventure-works.com scenario, can be delegated.

THOUGHT EXPERIMENT
Troubleshooting primary and secondary servers

In the following thought experiment, apply what you've learned about the "Design a Name Resolution Solution Strategy" objective. You can find answers to these questions in the "Answers" section at the end of this chapter.

You've configured a secure primary DNS server with a single zone, contoso.com, at a central data center and are deploying a new secondary server at a remote site. The secondary server has its DNS service configured but isn't receiving updates for the contoso.com DNS zone.

1. Describe troubleshooting steps that you can take on the secondary server as well as any additional configuration that may be necessary for this scenario to be successful.

2. Describe troubleshooting steps that you can take on the primary server as well as any additional configuration that may be necessary for this scenario to be successful.

MORE INFO **DNS HIERARCHY AND DELEGATION**

See *http://technet.microsoft.com/library/cc731879* for more information on the hierarchy and delegation concepts of DNS.

Objective summary

- The DNS service supports configurations to enhance security including DNSSEC, DNS socket pool, and cache locking.
- DNS socket pool randomizes the source port for DNS queries, and cache locking prevents cached entries from being overwritten for a certain percentage of their Time to Live (TTL) value.
- Microsoft's DNS implementation supports disjoint namespaces, in which the DNS name suffix varies from the Active Directory Domain Services (AD DS) domain name suffix.
- Zone delegation enables a different server to be authoritative for a given zone. This, coupled with zone hierarchy and application partitions, enables complex name service architectures for an organization.

Objective review

Answer the following questions to test your knowledge of the information in this objective. You can find the answers to these questions and explanations of why each answer choice is correct or incorrect in the "Answers" section at the end of this chapter.

1. Which of the following are supported disjoint namespace configurations in Windows Server 2012?

   A. When a suffix matches an Active Directory domain in the current or another forest

   B. In a multi–Active Directory domain forest with a single DNS namespace or zone

   C. In a single Active Directory domain that's split into multiple DNS zones

   D. When a certification authority (CA) domain member changes its DNS suffix

2. Which command creates an application partition?

   A. dnscmd <FQDN> /CreateDirectoryPartition <ServerName>

   B. dnscmd <ServerName> /CreateApplicationPartition <FQDN>

   C. dnscmd <ServerName> /CreateDirectoryPartition <FQDN>

   D. dnscmd <FQDN> /CreateApplicationPartition <ServerName>

3. Which feature of Microsoft's DNS implementation helps prevent cache poisoning?

   A. DNS socket pool

   B. Cache lock pooling

   C. Cache poisoning prevention

   D. DNS pool randomization

4. You've configured cache locking and have received reports that clients are receiving stale DNS query responses. Which registry key do you need to change in order to change the TTL ratio that remains locked?

   A. TTLRatioPercent

   B. CacheResetValue

   C. TTLLockingValue

   D. CacheLockingPercent

Objective 2.3: Design and manage an IP address management solution

Windows Server 2012 introduces a new feature called IP address management (IPAM) that helps administrators organize the infrastructure and hosts on the network. IPAM is a powerful tool that can be used to manage both IPv4 and IPv6 network infrastructure as well as provide auditing of an IP address space.

This objective covers the following topics:

- Design considerations, including IP address management technologies such as IPAM, Group Policy based, and manual provisioning, as well as distributed vs. centralized placement
- How to configure role-based access control
- How to configure IPAM auditing
- How to migrate IPs
- How to manage and monitor multiple DHCP and DNS servers
- How to configure data collection for IPAM

Design considerations for IP address management

When managing an IP address infrastructure, your overall goal is to reduce the administrative burden and overhead of managing the address space. For example, many organizations use something as simple as a spreadsheet for managing their address space. This makes tracking who makes changes to the address space difficult. Common tasks such as determining which devices use which IP need to be done manually and then updated manually. All this manual intervention for IP address management introduces errors, not to mention the overhead of having to do it in the first place.

In an ideal world, the IP address spaces in use would manage themselves as much as possible while requiring as little administrator intervention as possible. IP address management (IPAM) in Windows Server 2012 helps alleviate some of that overhead with several key features such as discovery, auditing, reporting, and monitoring.

IPAM enables IP address tracking for Windows Server 2008 and above domain controllers and network policy servers, enables some configuration and monitoring of DNS servers, and enables scope monitoring and configuration of DHCP servers. IPAM attempts to discover domain controllers, DNS servers, DHCP servers, and network policy servers at a regular interval. The servers themselves can be managed by IPAM or left unmanaged. However, to enable discovery, the server needs to allow communication from the IPAM server at the firewall level, and other security settings also need to allow the discovery to take place. All servers must reside in one Active Directory forest and must be domain members to be used with IPAM.

Designing an IPAM solution involves determining where to house the servers, whether at a central location or in a distributed fashion with an IPAM server at each site. IPAM servers don't communicate or share information with each other, but you can customize each server's scope to limit discovery to that site. The practical implication of this design choice is that you can allocate certain scopes in a multi-site environment so that they can be managed by a team local to that environment. In other environments, a centralized approach works best, but you can split IP address management as needed by your organization.

When deploying IPAM, you should be aware of the limitations for a single server:

- 150 DHCP servers
- 500 DNS servers
- 6000 DHCP scopes
- 150 DNS zones

Also, non-Microsoft devices such as routers and switches aren't managed or monitored by IPAM.

MORE INFO   **IPAM OVERVIEW**

See *http://technet.microsoft.com/library/hh831353* for an overview of IPAM, including additional limitations.

When installed, the IPAM server is provisioned manually or with Group Policy Objects (GPOs). The Provision IPAM Wizard walks through the provisioning process (see Figure 2-12). Note, however, that after you choose the provision method, you can't change it. Using the Group Policy Based option enables the servers to be marked as managed in a more automated fashion, and the GPOs can be removed when a server is marked as unmanaged.

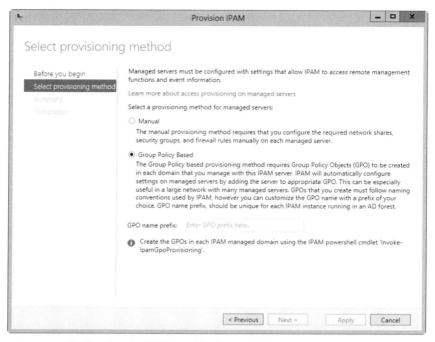

FIGURE 2-12 Configuring the IPAM provisioning method.

Through GPOs, you can add a Server Discovery task to the task scheduler but can also start it manually through the IPAM server manager. The types of servers to be discovered can also be configured, as shown in Figure 2-13.

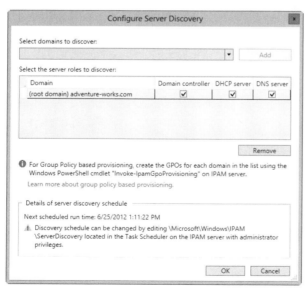

FIGURE 2-13 Configuring the types of servers to be discovered by IPAM.

When servers are discovered, their IPAM Access Status shows them as blocked, and their manageability will be Unspecified, as shown in Figure 2-14.

FIGURE 2-14 You need to correct the manageability status of a recently discovered server to be able to manage the server.

To configure the server so that it is manageable, add the appropriate GPOs to the server by running the following Windows PowerShell command (as Administrator) from the IPAM server:

```
Invoke-IpamGpoProvisioning -Domain <domain> -GpoPrefixName <Prefix> -IpamServerFqdn
<IPAM Server Name>
```

This command results in three GPOs being created. For example, if you use a GPO name prefix of IPAM1 when provisioning IPAM, the following Group Policy Objects would be created, which can be verified in the Group Policy Management tool:

- IPAM1_DC_NPS
- IPAM1_DNS
- IPAM1_DHCP

When this is complete, each server to be managed needs to obtain the GPOs. Run the following command from within the server itself:

```
gpupdate /force
```

The final step to manage the server is to set the server status to Managed. Right-click the server, select Edit Server, and set the Manageability status to Managed.

Configuring role-based access control

When installed, IPAM creates five security groups, as shown in Table 2-3. These groups are added during IPAM provisioning and can be used like other security groups in Windows. For example, adding users to one of these groups enables them to perform IPAM-related tasks according to the permissions for that group.

TABLE 2-3 Security groups created by IPAM

Security Group	Description
IPAM Users	Allows you to view information about the various areas being managed by IPAM with the exception of IP address-tracking information.
IPAM MSM Administrators	Includes the privileges in the IPAM Users group and adds the ability to manage the IPAM server.
IPAM ASM Administrators	Includes the privileges in the IPAM Users group and adds the ability to manage IP address space tasks and server management.
IPAM IP Audit Administrators	Views IP address-tracking information in addition to the privileges in the IMAP Users group.
IPAM Administrators	Makes up an overall administrative group that can perform all IPAM tasks.

Configuring IPAM auditing

IPAM can be used for auditing purposes to provide information on address utilization, policy compliance, and other information based on the type of servers being managed by IPAM. You use the Event Catalog to configure IPAM auditing (see Figure 2-15). The IP address audit functionality in IPAM collects user information along with the IP address, hostname, and client identifier (MAC address for IPv4 or DUID for IPv6). This information comes from managed DHCP servers, domain controllers, and network policy servers.

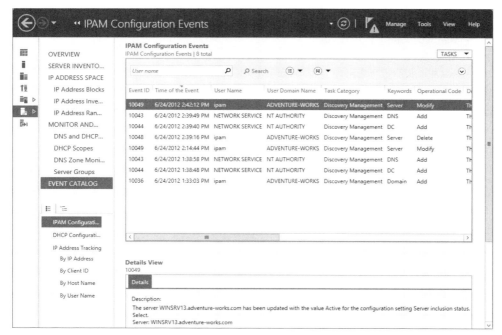

FIGURE 2-15 The Event Catalog in IPAM

By default, the IPAM configuration events are shown, but other events can be shown and can have reports created from the data within them. Included are query tools and a search box to help narrow the focus of the events displayed. Criteria can be added to a query filter, as shown in Figure 2-16.

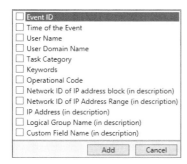

FIGURE 2-16 Additional filter criteria for IPAM auditing.

After the data is retrieved, it can be exported to a comma-separated value (CSV) file.

Migrating IP addresses

IPAM can help you manage IP addresses in a network. IPAM might be used to track utilization of IP addresses for a given site to ensure that enough addresses exist for clients at that site. IPAM defines IP address ranges as groups of contiguous IP addresses, and IP address blocks as groupings of IP address ranges.

When migrating IP addresses to be managed by IPAM, the addresses can be entered manually by address range, address block, and individually by address. You can also import IP addresses into IPAM with a CSV-formatted file. Figure 2-17 shows the Add Or Edit IPv4 Address Range dialog box.

FIGURE 2-17 Adding and editing an IP address range in IPAM.

The Managed By Service drop-down list is helpful for migration planning. With this dialog box you can select how the address block or range is now being managed from choices like IPAM (as shown), a non-Microsoft DHCP solution, Microsoft Virtual Machine Manager (VMM), or another method. Choosing this correctly then enables you to import the IP address space within IPAM but still have address assignment done using the current method. When ready, the IP address can be moved under IPAM management as appropriate.

Managing and monitoring multiple DHCP and DNS servers

IPAM can use logical groupings of servers for configuration, monitoring, and management. This is useful for managing a group of servers that are located at a remote site or have some other common criteria for management and monitoring in IPAM. Server groups are configured within the Monitor and Manage section of IPAM.

Within server groups in IPAM, you add a server group with the Add Server Group dialog box, shown in Figure 2-18.

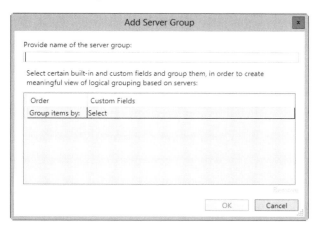

FIGURE 2-18 Adding a server group in IPAM.

As you see within Figure 2-18, you can also group servers by several criteria, as shown in Figure 2-19.

FIGURE 2-19 Criteria available for ordering the server group in IPAM.

Multi-filtering is available, such that you can choose to first group by one criterion and then additional criteria as needed to create a group with the necessary specificity.

After a server group is created, it can be found within the Server Groups section in the IPAM management console. Like other areas, server groups can be searched and their display order can be changed to locate the server group to be managed.

Configuring data collection

IPAM data-collection activities are scheduled using Task Scheduler and are run at regular intervals. The data collected depends on the items configured within IPAM. For example, if IPAM is being used to manage IP addresses, the data-collection activities include an IP address utilization scan for the IP addresses being managed. The length of time that it takes to collect data also varies accordingly.

The data-collection tasks are configured within the Task Scheduler Library under Microsoft | Windows | IPAM. Table 2-4 shows the task names and their default frequency.

TABLE 2-4 Default schedules for tasks in Task Scheduler

Task Name	Frequency
AddressExpiry	1 day
AddressUtilization	2 hours
Audit	1 day
ServerAvailability	15 minutes
ServerConfiguration	6 hours
ServerDiscovery	1 day
ServiceMonitoring	30 minutes

The type of server defines the data to be collected from that server. For example, DNS zones aren't collected from a DHCP server, and so on. You can change the data to be collected from a server within the Add Or Edit Server dialog box. Figure 2-20 shows this dialog box, within which the Server Type can be set according to the need for data collection.

THOUGHT EXPERIMENT
Configuring servers for IPAM management

In the following thought experiment, apply what you've learned about this objective. You can find answers to these questions in the "Answers" section at the end of this chapter.

You've installed the IPAM server role in a centralized placement and have configured it for GPO-based discovery. After the server discovery task, you see two servers available to manage.

Describe the steps involved to bring the servers under IPAM management.

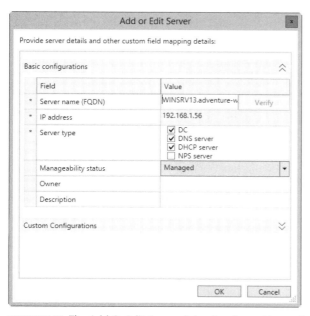

FIGURE 2-20 The Add Or Edit Server dialog box is used to configure the Server Type in IPAM.

MORE INFO   **CONFIGURING IPAM**

See *http://technet.microsoft.com/library/hh831622* for more information on configuring IPAM.

Objective summary

- IPAM has certain limitations on the number of servers that it can manage. These include 150 DHCP servers, 500 DNS servers, 150 DNS zones, and 6000 DHCP scopes.
- The IPAM server can locate servers to provision manually or by using Group Policy Objects (GPOs).
- IPAM servers can be distributed as appropriate for an organization's needs.
- IPAM creates several groups that can be used for role-based access control to the various functions in IPAM.
- IP addresses can be managed and audited in IPAM, and IPAM can be provisioned with IP addresses managed by other DHCP servers.
- Server groups help manage multiple servers in IPAM by creating logical groups as configured by administrators.
- Task Scheduler contains several tasks related to collection of data in IPAM, and data collection can be started manually.

Objective review

Answer the following questions to test your knowledge of the information in this objective. You can find the answers to these questions and explanations of why each answer choice is correct or incorrect in the "Answers" section at the end of this chapter.

1. You need to grant access for viewing audit information within IPAM. To which group should you add a user to, to grant that user the minimum level of permission for this task?

   A. IPAM Users

   B. IPAM IP Address Audit Admins

   C. IPAM Administrators

   D. IPAM IP Audit Administrators

2. When provisioning IPAM servers using GPOs, servers are discovered. After configuring them to be managed in IPAM, what command do you need to run on the server to be managed?

   A. Invoke-IpamAudit /server <ipam-servername> /domain

   B. gpupdate /reset

   C. Invoke-IpamAudit /server <ipam-servername> /configure

   D. gpupdate /force

3. What is the default data-collection interval for the ServerDiscovery task?

   A. 3 days

   B. 8 hours

   C. 1 day

   D. 1 hour

4. Which of the following isn't a valid criterion for grouping events (assuming you're not using a custom criterion)?

   A. Keywords

   B. Event Region

   C. User Name

   D. User Domain Name

5. When do IPAM servers exchange information on the servers under their respective management?

    A. When configured in a distributed scenario

    B. Never; IPAM servers don't exchange information

    C. When configured with System Center 2012

    D. When configured to use DNS

Chapter summary

- The DHCP server role in Windows Server 2012 provides for redundancy with split scope, failover through hot standby and load sharing, and failover clustering.
- Failover clustering enables both servers to assign DHCP information by sharing the same DHCP database on a shared storage location.
- DHCP filtering configures how the server to responds to clients by using link-layer MAC addresses.
- The DHCP Management Pack, part of System Center Operations Manager, enables monitoring and reporting of the DHCP service.
- The DNS service supports configurations to enhance security including DNSSEC, DNS socket pool, and cache locking.
- You can manage and audit IP addresses in IPAM. You also can provision IPAM with IP addresses that are managed by other DHCP servers.

Answers

This section contains the solutions to the thought experiments and answers to the objective review questions in this chapter.

Objective 2.1: Thought experiment

You would likely use Hot Standby Failover deploying two servers. The server at the primary location would normally service clients at the primary location, and a secondary server at a remote location would service requests for the remote site. In a Hot Standby scenario, if one of the servers fails, the other can service requests for its failed partner.

Objective 2.1: Review

1. **Correct answer:** C

   A. **Incorrect:** This isn't the correct split as recommended.

   B. **Incorrect:** This isn't the correct split as recommended.

   C. **Correct:** An 80 percent/20 percent ratio for split scopes is good practice, with the primary server receiving 80 percent of the addresses and the secondary server receiving 20 percent.

   D. **Incorrect:** This isn't the correct split as recommended.

2. **Correct answers:** A and B

   A. **Correct:** 00-11-09-*-*-* is a valid filter using wildcards to match multiple MACs.

   B. **Correct:** 001109001111 is a valid MAC filter.

   C. **Incorrect:** 00:11:09:09:11:09 isn't a valid MAC filter; it uses colons as a separator.

   D. **Incorrect:** 00-11-09-7c-ef-% isn't a valid MAC filter; it uses a percent sign as a wildcard indicator.

3. **Correct answer:** A

   A. **Correct:** The path C:\Windows\system32\dhcp is the default location for the database. This is configured in the DHCP server's Properties sheet.

   B. **Incorrect:** The path C:\Program Files\Microsoft\DHCP\Data doesn't exist.

   C. **Incorrect:** The path C:\Windows\system32\DHCP\Data doesn't exist.

   D. **Incorrect:** The registry key HKEY_LOCAL_MACHINE\SOFTWARE\Microsoft\DHCP doesn't house the DHCP database.

4. **Correct answer:** B

   A. **Incorrect:** Increasing the split ratio so that the secondary server has more IP addresses from the scope makes it only so that the secondary server can assign more addresses; it doesn't help alleviate the issue of the secondary server assigning addresses to clients at the primary location.

   B. **Correct:** Introducing a delay for DHCP offers from the secondary using the DHCP management console accomplishes this task by allowing the primary server to respond first but the secondary to respond after a period of time. Because DHCP clients accept the first response, this achieves the requirements.

   C. **Incorrect:** Reducing the load on the primary server so that it can respond faster may help, but because the scenario doesn't indicate that the primary server was overloaded, the secondary server may just be responding faster for other reasons.

   D. **Incorrect:** Placing the secondary DHCP server on a different network segment to introduce a delay in the response doesn't meet the requirement and may introduce connectivity problems for DHCP responses.

Objective 2.2: Thought experiment

1. On the secondary server, you should make sure that the primary server is reachable. This might be achieved with a simple ping command, assuming that ICMP echo requests and echo responses aren't blocked by a firewall. You could also use nslookup on the secondary server and point to the primary server to query for information on the contoso.com domain.

2. On the primary server, you should ensure network connectivity to the secondary server and—importantly—ensure that zone transfers are allowed to the secondary server. This is accomplished at the zone level within the Zone Transfers tab of the Properties sheet. Ensuring that the firewall allows both UDP and TCP ports 53 inbound is also a good idea.

Objective 2.2: Review

1. **Correct answers:** B and C.

   A. **Incorrect:** This isn't a supported configuration as defined by Microsoft.

   B. **Correct:** This is a supported configuration.

   C. **Correct:** This is a supported configuration

   D. **Incorrect:** This isn't a supported configuration.

2. **Correct answer:** C

   A. **Incorrect:** The dnscmd command syntax is incorrect.

   B. **Incorrect:** The dnscmd command syntax is incorrect.

   C. **Correct:** This is the correct syntax for this task.

   D. **Incorrect:** The dnscmd command syntax is incorrect.

3. **Correct answer:** A

   A. **Correct:** DNS socket pool randomizes source ports for queries.

   B. **Incorrect:** This isn't a valid option.

   C. **Incorrect:** This isn't a valid option.

   D. **Incorrect:** This isn't a valid option.

4. **Correct answer:** D

   A. **Incorrect:** This isn't a valid registry key.

   B. **Incorrect:** This isn't a valid registry key.

   C. **Incorrect:** This isn't a valid registry key.

   D. **Correct:** This is the correct registry key.

Objective 2.3: Thought experiment

You first need create the GPOs by using the Invoke-IpamGpoProvisioning command. Then, you need to run gpupdate /force on the servers to be managed. Finally, you need to set the server to Managed status within IPAM.

Objective 2.3: Review

1. **Correct answer:** D

   A. **Incorrect:** IPAM Users is a real group but doesn't include the permission to view audit information.

   B. **Incorrect:** This isn't a real group.

   C. **Incorrect:** The IPAM Administrators group has the privilege but isn't the minimum level necessary for the task.

   D. **Correct:** IPAM IP Audit Administrators is the minimum privileges required for this task.

2. **Correct answer:** D

   A. **Incorrect:** This isn't a real command.

   B. **Incorrect:** Although gpupdate is a real command, the proposed answer shows an invalid switch for this operation.

   C. **Incorrect:** This is an invalid command.

   D. **Correct:** The gpupdate /force command retrieves the appropriate GPOs from the IPAM server.

3. **Correct answer:** C

   A. **Incorrect:** This interval is invalid for this task.

   B. **Incorrect:** This interval is invalid for this task.

   C. **Correct:** The ServerDiscovery task runs once daily through Task Scheduler by default.

   D. **Incorrect:** This interval is invalid for this task.

4. **Correct answer:** B

   A. **Incorrect:** This is a valid criterion; refer to Figure 2-16.

   B. **Correct:** Event Region isn't a valid criterion.

   C. **Incorrect:** This is a valid criterion; refer to Figure 2-16.

   D. **Incorrect:** This is a valid criterion; refer to Figure 2-16.

5. **Correct answer:** B

   A. **Incorrect:** IPAM servers don't exchange information.

   B. **Correct:** IPAM servers don't communicate to exchange information.

   C. **Incorrect:** IPAM servers don't communicate using this protocol.

   D. **Incorrect:** IPAM servers don't exchange information.

CHAPTER 3

Design and implement network access services

This chapter is about providing safe and secure access to your network resources. Beginning with VPN solution design, continuing to DirectAccess, and then focusing on Network Access Protection (NAP), this chapter heavily leans toward solution design. However, implementation of those solutions is also featured.

Objectives in this chapter:

- Objective 3.1: Design a VPN solution
- Objective 3.2: Design a DirectAccess solution
- Objective 3.3: Implement a scalable Remote Access solution
- Objective 3.4: Design a network protection solution
- Objective 3.5: Implement a network protection solution

Objective 3.1: Design a VPN solution

Virtual private network (VPN) solutions have evolved over the years. Windows Server 2012 extends the usage of DirectAccess and makes deploying it even easier in both simple and complex topologies. This objective examines some of the considerations for design of a VPN solution with Windows Server 2012.

This objective covers the following topics:
- VPN design considerations
- Security certificate deployment
- Firewall design considerations
- Client and site-to-site considerations
- Bandwidth and protocol implications
- VPN deployment configurations with CMAK

VPN design considerations

Designing a VPN solution means ensuring secure and reliable connectivity to network resources. This section focuses on configuring security certificates, firewall, bandwidth usage, and protocols used in the VPN solution.

Remote Access is configured as a role in Windows Server 2012. DirectAccess management has been combined with the traditional Routing and Remote Access Service (RRAS) VPN solution to make management easier and provide the best level of support for the most clients. When the role is installed, several other components are installed, such as the Remote Access Service (RAS) Connection Manager Administration Kit (CMAK) and Internet Information Service (IIS). Windows Server 2012 makes deploying a remote access solution easier with the help of the new Remote Access Getting Started Wizard.

> **MORE INFO**   **VPN PROTOCOLS**
>
> You should be comfortable with the protocol-level of VPNs, including their levels of and requirements for security and their compatibility with various versions of Windows and non-Windows clients. See *http://technet.microsoft.com/en-us/library/cc771298.aspx* for more information on the protocols and *http://technet.microsoft.com/en-us/library/cc725734.aspx* for an overview of the configuration that contains links to additional information.

An important step in designing a VPN solution is to plan the overall infrastructure. Included in this step is deciding where the Remote Access server should be placed within the network topology and how it should be configured. You can configure Remote Access with one or two network adapters. If the server is configured with one network adapter, it likely will be behind a network address translation (NAT) device connected to the internal network. If the server is configured with two network adapters, the server can be configured in an edge scenario with one adapter connected to the external or perimeter network (behind a NAT device or a firewall) and the other adapter connected to the internal network.

When integrating DirectAccess, you need to keep in mind additional addressing considerations because DirectAccess uses IPv6 with IPsec. However, because IPv6 isn't a requirement, translation services such as 6to4, Teredo, IP-HTTPS, NAT64, and ISATAP automatically provide compatibility for IPv4 networks. These translation technologies have specific firewall considerations, as discussed later in this objective.

> **MORE INFO**   **IPV6 TRANSITION TECHNOLOGIES**
>
> For more information on IPv6 transition technologies, see *http://technet.microsoft.com/library/bb726951.aspx*.

Security certificate deployment

Certificate deployment involves several planning stages, including planning the computer name and adding a static IP, both which would likely already be done in an enterprise-level deployment. Other steps include the configuration of the certificate authority itself.

> **MORE INFO   PLANNING FOR CERTIFICATE DEPLOYMENT**
>
> See *http://technet.microsoft.com/library/jj125370* for more information on the planning considerations for certificate deployment.

Three scenarios are identified for certificates as they relate to Remote Access:

- IPsec authentication
- IP-HTTPS server
- Network location server

IPsec certificate considerations

IPsec authentication uses an internal certificate authority (CA). The internal CA issues certificates to both the clients and the Remote Access server. With DirectAccess in Windows Server 2012, the Remote Access server can proxy Kerberos requests over Secure Sockets Layer (SSL), thus making the use of IPsec no longer a requirement for this scenario. However, multisite deployments cannot use Kerberos proxying and therefore must use certificates for this scenario.

When certificates are used for IPsec, the following requirements and recommendations are noted:

- An enterprise CA should be set up.
- Group policy–based auto enrollment should be used to ensure that all domain members receive the certificate from an enterprise CA.
- The certificate needs to have client authentication Extended Key Usage (EKU).
- The trust chains for the client and server certificates should connect to the same root certificate, which is configured in the DirectAccess configuration.

When installed, Remote Access listens for HTTPS requests and, as a result, requires a certificate for this communication. A public CA signs the certificate for the IP-HTTPS scenario, but an internal CA or self-signed certificate can also work, assuming that the Certificate Revocation List (CRL) distribution point is available to external clients.

IP-HTTPS certificate considerations

A public CA certificate should be used for HTTPS-based Remote Access so that clients have the best compatibility. Also, the subject field of the certificate should specify the IPv4 address or the Fully Qualified Domain Name (FQDN) of the Remote Access server, and the common name of the certificate should match the name of the site or use a wildcard certificate. The EKU field should use the Server Authentication object identifier. The certificate must be imported into the personal store.

Network location server certificate considerations

The certificate should use the IP address or FQDN of the network location URL for the Subject field in the certificate, and the EKU field uses the Server Authentication object identifier.

Firewall design considerations

Firewall design considerations depend largely on the protocol and IP version involved in the Remote Access solution. For example, if the Remote Access server is IPv4-based, certain firewall exceptions are required, as listed in Table 3-1.

TABLE 3-1 Firewall Exceptions

Exception	Reason
User Datagram Protocol (UDP) inbound/outbound port 3544	Teredo
Internet Protocol 41 inbound/outbound	6to4
Transmission Control Protocol (TCP) inbound port 62000	Remote Access deployed with a single network adapter with the network location server

Remote Access servers using IPv6 have the exceptions listed in Table 3-2.

TABLE 3-2 Remote Access Server Exceptions

Exception	Reason
Internet Protocol 50	IPv6 traffic
UDP inbound/outbound port 500	IPv6 traffic
ICMPv6 inbound/outbound	Teredo

Other firewalls should also allow traffic for Internet Protocol 41 for ISATAP as well as TCP/UDP for IPv4 and IPv6 traffic between the Remote Access server and the client. If Teredo is being used, Internet Control Message Protocol (ICMP) should also be allowed.

Client and site-to-site considerations

Remote Access and VPN solutions are used not only to connect clients and traditional information workers to their corporate network, but also to connect sites or data centers to each other. This can be done to provide redundancy. When used for redundancy, the Remote Access server has two network adapters, each connected to a different Internet service provider (ISP). The sites can then have tunnels created between them.

Windows Server 2012 enables multiple entry points for DirectAccess solutions. The entry point used by the client is determined manually by the client, by a global load balancer, or by an automatic probe based on proximity.

When deploying a multisite entry-point scenario, each site is associated with a single Active Directory site for authentication. The Active Directory site should have a read-only domain controller. However, each site isn't required to have its own Active Directory site. Multiple entry points can connect to a central Active Directory site, as might be the case in which multiple entry points are defined based on geography but have a single central data center acting as the Active Directory site.

Bandwidth and protocol implications

When deploying a Remote Access solution, you should consider whether to support clients that cannot use DirectAccess. If this is the case, you need to provide a traditional VPN solution. When you use the Remote Access Setup Wizard, you choose how these clients are authenticated, and your design should reflect the planning involved.

DirectAccess clients use a *network location server*, a website used to help a client determine whether it's currently connected to the internal network. Therefore, clients must also be able to resolve the address of the network location server using DNS.

VPN deployment configurations with CMAK

The Connection Manager Administration Kit (CMAK) enables you to create a customized connection experience for clients using a VPN solution. Within the CMAK you can customize the connection such that the end users don't need to enter the IP address of the VPN server. CMAK offers complex and granular control so that you can provide a customized support telephone number, should your users need assistance when using the connection. VPN support is configured on the Add Support for VPN Connections dialog box within the Connection Manager Administration Kit Wizard. This dialog box, shown in Figure 3-1, enables you to specify the IP address for the VPN server or to allow the user to choose a VPN server.

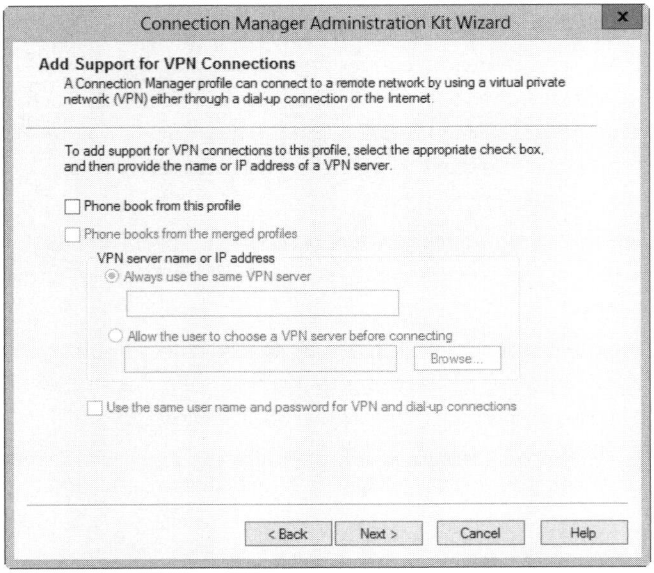

FIGURE 3-1 Adding support for a VPN connection to a profile created with CMAK.

The Connection Manager Administration Kit Wizard also enables you to modify the VPN entry with several options through the New VPN Entry dialog box, as shown in Figure 3-2.

FIGURE 3-2 Configuring a new VPN entry as part of CMAK.

Within this dialog box, on the IPv4 tab, you can configure the client's DNS and WINS configuration, specify whether to use IP header compression, and indicate whether to make the connection the client's default gateway. You can configure DNS and the default gateway on the IPv6 tab, the DNS suffix and whether to register the address in DNS on the Advanced tab, and several security-related configuration items on the Security tab (see Figure 3-3).

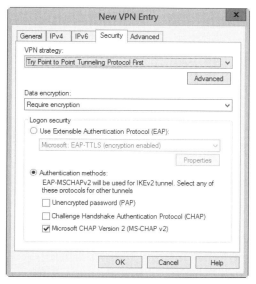

FIGURE 3-3 Configuring VPN-related security options in CMAK.

MORE INFO   **CMAK**

See *http://technet.microsoft.com/library/hh831675* for more information on CMAK.

THOUGHT EXPERIMENT
IPsec-based solution

In the following thought experiment, apply what you've learned about this objective. You can find answers to these questions in the "Answers" section at the end of this chapter.

You are deploying an IPsec-based solution for your organization. For part of that deployment, you need to design the certificate infrastructure for the solution.

What types of certificates should be used for this scenario?

Objective summary

- Designing a VPN solution with Windows Server 2012 involves choosing how clients connect to the network.
- For clients that can support DirectAccess, Windows Server 2012 offers many powerful features. However, older clients and non-Windows–based clients can still use VPN solutions with a Remote Access server.
- Certificate deployment comes with several recommendations, depending on the protocol used for the configuration. For example, IP-HTTPS configurations should use a public CA, while other solutions can use internal CAs, assuming that a Certificate Revocation List (CRL) distribution point is available.
- Firewall considerations also depend on the protocols and solution in use, specifically around whether IPv4 or IPv6 is used, but also including tools such as DirectAccess.
- You can use the Connection Manager Administration Kit (CMAK) to create a custom VPN profile for clients to use when connecting to the corporate network. You can customize many aspects of the VPN connection using CMAK.

Objective review

Answer the following questions to test your knowledge of the information in this objective. You can find the answers to these questions and explanations of why each answer choice is correct or incorrect in the "Answers" section at the end of this chapter.

1. You need to deploy an IPv4-based Teredo solution. In the firewall, which protocol and ports should be allowed for Teredo?

    A. TCP/3544

    B. TCP/62000

    C. UDP/3544

    D. TCP/443

2. Which of the following isn't identified as a certificate scenario for Remote Access?

    A. IP-HTTPS

    B. PPTP

    C. IPsec

    D. Network location server

3. What information should the EKU field on a certificate store?

   A. The Server Authentication object identifier

   B. The common name or wildcard of the IPsec server

   C. The Server Name OID

   D. The IP address of the Remote Access server

Objective 3.2: Design a DirectAccess solution

DirectAccess provides an advanced remote access option for Windows-based clients. Windows Server 2012 eases the deployment of DirectAccess and provides a Getting Started Wizard to help automate much of the deployment.

DirectAccess frequently works alongside traditional VPN technology such that Windows clients capable of using DirectAccess (Windows 7 and above) can do so while other clients can use the VPN to access corporate resources. Windows Server 2012 enables a unified remote access solution with both DirectAccess and Remote Access server and with VPN running through the same management console.

A key concept when deploying DirectAccess is the use of tunnels, specifically split or force tunnels. With a split tunnel, clients connect to corporate resources through the tunnel coupled to the corporate network, and connect to Internet resources through their normal network connection. With a force tunnel, clients use the corporate tunnel for all communication, both to the corporate network and to the Internet.

Before Windows Server 2012, you had to configure the force-tunnel scenario by using Group Policy. However, you can now configure force tunneling in the Remote Access Management Console.

This objective covers the following topics:

- Designing a DirectAccess topology
- Migrating from Forefront UAG
- Deploying DirectAccess
- Using enterprise certificates

Designing a DirectAccess topology

When designing a topology for DirectAccess, you should consider which resources need to be available to clients. The location of those resources within the network is also vital for designing a DirectAccess topology. For example, if certain internal resources can't work with DirectAccess, you might need to look to a different topology than if you have a native Windows Server 2012 data center.

Table 3-3 lists three scenarios for DirectAccess deployment.

TABLE 3-3 DirectAccess deployment scenarios

Deployment scenario	Description
Full Intranet Access	Similar to a VPN in which authentication and traffic between an external client and the edge of the network is encrypted but internal traffic is unencrypted; no end-to-end protection for data or authentication.
Selected Server Access	Traffic between the client and the DirectAccess server is encrypted and authentication data is provided to the internal server resources. However, internal traffic isn't encrypted.
End-to-End Access	All traffic is encrypted and authentication data is provided to internal servers. The IPsec connection for the traffic is made directly between the client and the internal application server.

DirectAccess uses IPv6 for communication between clients and endpoints. Most topologies involve some type of transition technology, such as Intra-Site Automatic Tunnel Addressing Protocol (ISATAP). Applications and operating systems participating in DirectAccess also need to be IPv6-capable. For environments, applications, or operating systems limited to IPv4 only, NAT64/DNS64 service must be provided.

> **MORE INFO DIRECTACCESS DESIGN DOCUMENT**
>
> Microsoft has an extensive DirectAccess design document available at *http://www.microsoft.com/download/details.aspx?id=23801*, which provides more information on design considerations, including ones not listed as objectives for the 70-413 exam.

Migrating from Forefront UAG

Migrating from Forefront UAG DirectAccess to DirectAccess running on Windows Server 2012 comes in two scenarios: a side-by-side migration and an offline migration. During the design phase of your DirectAccess deployment, you primarily need to consider which scenario is most appropriate for your organization. The side-by-side migration has the least impact on availability but requires more administrative overhead to configure and maintain both servers simultaneously, whereas the offline migration scenario is an all-or-nothing approach.

Side-by-side migration

A side-by-side migration calls for both the Forefront UAG DirectAccess server and the new Windows Server 2012 DirectAccess server to run simultaneously. When the Windows Server 2012 DirectAccess server is deployed, clients begin using that server. In this scenario, each server uses different settings such as IP addresses, host names, and the like so that clients can connect to each server running side by side.

Side-by-side migration involves four steps:

1. Export configuration settings from Forefront UAG.

2. Record all Group Policy Objects (GPOs) in use for Forefront UAG.

3. Install the Remote Access role on the Windows Server 2012 server.

4. Configure the Remote Access server, including GPOs.

> **MORE INFO** **SIDE-BY-SIDE MIGRATION**
>
> See *http://technet.microsoft.com/library/hh831643* for more specific steps and information on the side-by-side migration scenario.

Offline migration

In an offline migration scenario, the Forefront UAG server is turned off before the Windows Server 2012 DirectAccess server is deployed. In such a scenario, the existing server settings like IP address, host name, and certificates can be used on the new server. This scenario is sometimes informally called a *big bang migration* because all clients must be migrated at the same time.

After you take the existing server offline, you use the following overall steps to complete the offline migration:

1. Install the Remote Access role on Windows Server 2012.

2. Configure IP addresses to match the legacy Forefront UAG server.

3. Install a certificate for IP-HTTPS connections.

4. Prepare GPOs for the Remote Access server.

5. Configure DirectAccess.

> **MORE INFO** **OFFLINE MIGRATION**
>
> See *http://technet.microsoft.com/en-us/library/hh831673* for more information and specific steps related to the offline migration scenario.

Deploying DirectAccess

Previous versions of DirectAccess required a full Public Key Infrastructure (PKI) deployment. DirectAccess in Windows Server 2012 no longer has this requirement, and you can now accomplish deployment by using the Getting Started Wizard, which you'll see later in this chapter.

Prior versions of DirectAccess also required IPv6-capable operating systems and applications. However, DirectAccess in Windows Server 2012 now includes fully integrated NAT64 and DNS64 translation technologies, making it possible to use DirectAccess even with applications and operating systems that aren't IPv6 capable.

You can now deploy DirectAccess behind a NAT device and have support for multiple domains, load balancing, and multiple sites. These changes with DirectAccess in Windows Server 2012 alter the design possibilities for DirectAccess significantly. For example, before Windows Server 2012, the DirectAccess server needed to have two network interfaces with two consecutive public IPv4 addresses. This is no longer the case; NAT support makes it possible to deploy the DirectAccess server inside the corporate network.

> **NOTE   NLB LIMITATIONS FOR DIRECTACCESS**
>
> The Network Load Balancing (NLB) capabilities of DirectAccess in Windows Server 2012 are limited to eight nodes, and the application doesn't provide true cluster-aware capabilities. In other words, if one server involved in the NLB goes offline, existing connections to that machine aren't automatically transferred to other servers involved in the NLB configuration.

> **MORE INFO   NEW DIRECTACCESS FEATURES**
>
> See *http://technet.microsoft.com/library/hh831416* for more information on the new features of DirectAccess in Windows Server 2012.

Table 3-4 lists the planning steps for DirectAccess deployment.

TABLE 3-4 Planning for DirectAccess deployment

Planning Step	Description
Client Access	Determine how clients will access the DirectAccess server and how Network Connectivity Assistant (NCA) or DirectAccess Connectivity Assistant (DCA) will be deployed.
Remote Access Server Deployment	Examine options for deployment of the servers involved in Remote Access.
Infrastructure Server Deployment	Plan how other servers involved in the DirectAccess deployment will interact. These include servers such as DNS and network location servers.
Application Server Deployment	Examine how application servers will interact with the deployment and what authentication is necessary for the clients accessing the application servers.

Using enterprise certificates

DirectAccess in Windows Server 2012 removes the requirement for PKI infrastructure. In its place, DirectAccess in Windows Server 2012 uses a Kerberos proxy running over HTTPS— meaning that a standard SSL certificate can be used for this deployment scenario. The certificate presumably is signed by a trusted certificate authority (CA) that is trusted by the clients, but a self-signed certificate can also be used. DirectAccess also can generate the self-signed certificate during deployment. One scenario in which a PKI deployment is required is in the case of two-factor authentication using Smart Cards or One-Time Passwords (OTPs).

To use Multisite Remote Access, IPsec authentication must be set to client certificates. This setting is configured within the Authentication page in the Remote Access Setup Wizard (see Figure 3-4).

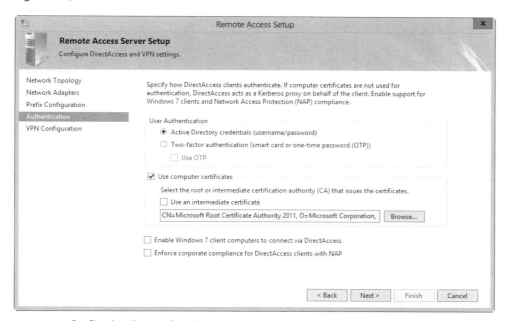

FIGURE 3-4 Configuring IPsec authentication to use a trusted root CA.

MORE INFO **CONFIGURING CERTIFICATES**

See *http://technet.microsoft.com/en-us/library/jj134204#ConfigCAs* for more information on certificate configuration as it relates to DirectAccess.

THOUGHT EXPERIMENT
Migrating to Windows Server 2012

In the following thought experiment, apply what you've learned about this objective. You can find answers to these questions in the "Answers" section at the end of this chapter.

You now have a Windows Server 2008 R2 deployment of Forefront UAG DirectAccess in a single data center. You'll be upgrading to Windows Server 2012 across the entire data center along with Windows 8 clients. First, you upgrade all application and infrastructure servers, followed by the clients. Then, you migrate the DirectAccess server.

1. Describe the migration scenario that you should use for DirectAccess.

2. Describe the DirectAccess deployment scenario that you should choose for this environment.

Objective summary

- DirectAccess involves three access scenarios: end-to-end, selected server, and full intranet access.

- Forefront UAG DirectAccess provides two primary migration scenarios: side-by-side and offline.

- Side-by-side migration has additional overhead but doesn't require the downtime that an offline migration does.

- DirectAccess in Windows Server 2012 can operate without a PKI deployment within the organization.

- Deploying DirectAccess involves four primary steps: client configuration, server configuration, infrastructure configuration, and application server configuration.

Objective review

Answer the following questions to test your knowledge of the information in this objective. You can find the answers to these questions and explanations of why each answer choice is correct or incorrect in the "Answers" section at the end of this chapter.

1. In which step of DirectAccess deployment do you configure things such as the DNS server and related servers to be used by DirectAccess clients?

   A. Infrastructure deployment

   B. Application server deployment

   C. Client configuration deployment

   D. DNS server deployment

2. This type of migration from Forefront UAG has the least downtime.

   A. Offline

   B. Intraserver

   C. Side-by-side

   D. End–to-end

3. What is the minimum number of network interfaces required for DirectAccess in Windows Server 2012 so that it can be deployed behind NAT?

   A. Two

   B. One

   C. Three

   D. Six

Objective 3.3: Implement a scalable Remote Access solution

This objective brings you from the design aspects involved in network access services into the configuration of the solutions.

This objective covers the following topics:

- Configuring site-to-site VPN
- Configuring packet filters
- Implementing packet tracing
- Implementing multisite Remote Access
- Configuring Remote Access clustered with Network Load Balancing (NLB)
- Configuring DirectAccess

Configuring site-to-site VPN

Site-to-site VPN is enabled in the Remote Access Management Console in Windows Server 2012. Clicking Enable Site-To-Site VPN in the Configuration task pane launches a wizard for configuring the settings for site-to-site VPN.

During configuration, the wizard retrieves and then sets on the server such information as any applied Group Policy Objects as well as DirectAccess and VPN configuration. When complete, the wizard reports the results, as shown in Figure 3-5.

FIGURE 3-5 The results of configuring site-to-site VPN in Windows Server 2012.

As you can see from these results, warnings indicate that the Remote Access (remoteaccess) service needs to be restarted for the changes to take effect.

Configuring packet filters

Packet filters refer to the firewall rules enabled for various components of DirectAccess and VPNs. The packet filters necessary for a given DirectAccess or VPN installation depend on what's been deployed. This section examines some configuration items related to packet filters in general.

> **MORE INFO** **USING PACKET FILTERS IN REMOTE ACCESS CONFIGURATIONS**
>
> See *http://technet.microsoft.com/library/ee382294* for a more thorough overview on packet filters as they apply to Remote Access configurations.

You configure packet filters in the Windows Firewall with Advanced Security console. Three sets of rules apply to a given Remote Access configuration: Inbound, Outbound, and Connection Security. The Inbound and Outbound rules are common firewall rules applied for ports and protocols involved in Remote Access. When installed, DirectAccess configures the packet filters according to the deployment chosen in the Getting Started Wizard or Remote Access Setup Wizard.

Implementing packet tracing

To enable packet tracing, click Start Tracing in the dashboard's Monitoring task pane of the Remote Access Management Console. Doing so reveals the Start Tracing dialog box, as shown in Figure 3-6.

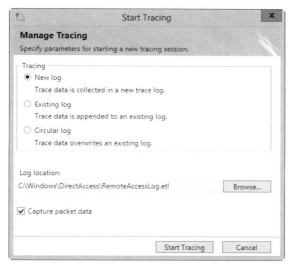

FIGURE 3-6 Implementing packet tracing in Remote Access.

As you can see from Figure 3-6, the trace log has three settings: New Log, Existing Log, and Circular Log. Creating a new log does just that—it creates a new log. The Existing Log setting appends to an existing log, and Circular Log overwrites an existing log.

To stop tracing, click Stop Tracing within the Remote Access Management Console.

Implementing Multisite Remote Access

Multisite Remote Access is found in the Configuration section of the Remote Access Management Console. The Enable Multisite task within Multisite Deployment in the task pane starts the Enable Multisite Deployment Wizard, which guides you through the process of configuring Multisite Remote Access.

For deployment of Multisite Remote Access, both the Network Location Server and the IP-HTTPS server must use trusted certificates and cannot use self-signed certificates.

The Enable Multisite Deployment Wizard begins with configuration related to the multisite deployment name and the first entry point (see Figure 3-7).

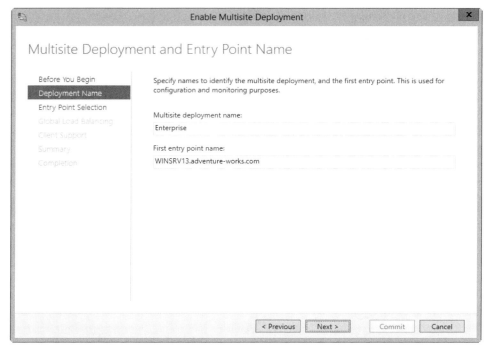

FIGURE 3-7 Beginning the Enable Multisite Deployment Wizard.

The wizard's next step enables you to choose how clients can find the best entry point:

- Assign entry points automatically and allow clients to select manually
- Assign entry points automatically only

The next step of the Enable Multisite Deployment Wizard (shown in Figure 3-8) deals with load balancing.

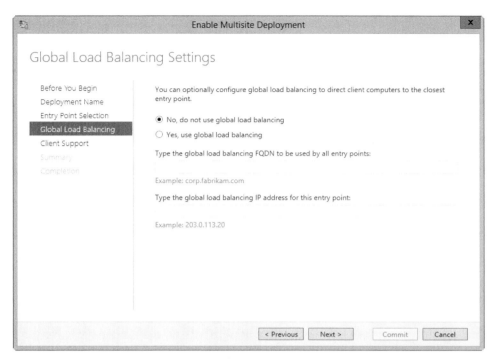

FIGURE 3-8 Choosing the load-balancing configuration as it relates to a multisite deployment.

Figure 3-9 shows the wizard's Client Support pane, where you choose whether to support Windows 8 clients on the deployment or if down-level Windows 7 computers should be allowed as well.

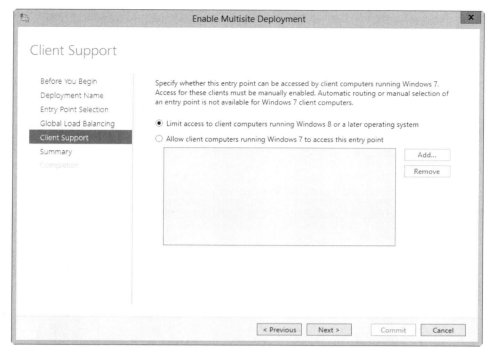

FIGURE 3-9 Choosing the level of client support for a multisite deployment.

After you configure the initial deployment, you typically perform additional configuration, such as add another entry point. This is accomplished through the Add an Entry Point Wizard.

> **NOTE** **ADDING ENTRY POINTS**
>
> The Remote Access server role must be configured on the server to be added to the multisite configuration. However, Remote Access should not be configured on that new server. In other words, the Getting Started Wizard cannot have been run on the new server. If it has, the Add an Entry Point Wizard can't get past step 1 and returns an error indicating that the new server has already been configured.

The Add an Entry Point Wizard first gathers the name of the server to be added to the multisite deployment. After that, the network topology is gathered, followed by the name that the clients use to contact this entry point. The network adapters are configured next (see Figure 3-10). This pane enables you to choose the network adapter to be used for the entry point along with the appropriate IP-HTTPS certificate.

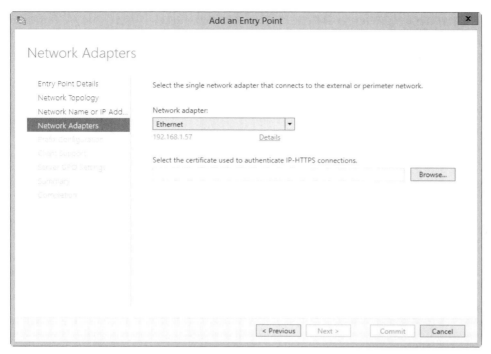

FIGURE 3-10 Choosing network adapter settings when adding an entry point to a multisite deployment.

Client support is next in the wizard (similar to Figure 3-9), and finally the GPO settings, which are typically left at their default settings. With that, the entry point is configured and can then be managed through the Remote Access Management Console on the server on which the multisite deployment is configured.

You can also change the settings for the multisite deployment through the Configure Multisite Settings dialog box, which provides a wizard-like interface to reconfigure many of the settings configured during initial deployment. Disabling a multisite deployment requires all the entry points to first be removed. This is accomplished within each entry point's Configuration Summary.

However, if the entry point to be removed exists on a Remote Access server that's currently being managed by this server, you can't simply click Remove Entry Point. Instead, you must first select Manage a Remote Server to begin the process of removing the entry point. This is true only for Remote Access servers managed by this server, not for servers that are simply members of the multisite deployment.

> **MORE INFO** **TEST LAB GUIDE**
>
> Microsoft has a test lab guide for multisite access available at *http://technet.microsoft.com/library/hh831461*.

Configuring Remote Access clustered with NLB

Network Load Balancing (NLB) can be used for Remote Access to provide greater availability and to enable the load to be shared among more than one server. NLB must be installed as a feature through the Add Roles and Features Wizard before enabling it in Remote Access.

To configure NLB, invoke the Enable Load Balancing Wizard from the Configuration section of the Remote Access Management Console. This wizard verifies settings and enables you to set the dedicated IP (DIP) to be used for the load-balanced cluster for both IPv4 and IPv6. Two special configuration items that might be different for a deployment include the IPv6 Prefix, which must be 59 for the load-balancing configuration, and the IP Address Assignment.

The prefix is configured on the Prefix Configuration pane of the Remote Access Setup Wizard, as shown in Figure 3-11.

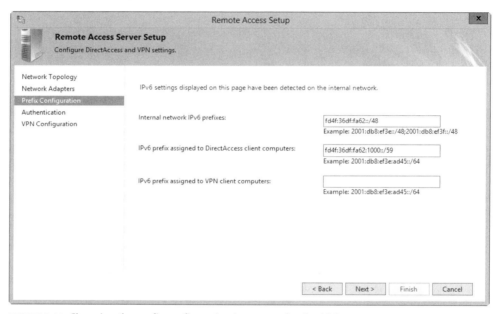

FIGURE 3-11 Changing the prefix configuration in preparation for NLB.

The IP Address Assignment is configured in the VPN Configuration pane of the Remote Access Setup Wizard, as shown in Figure 3-12.

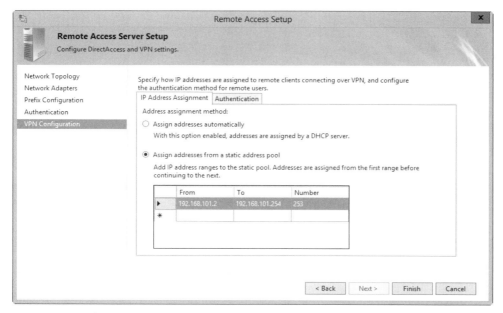

FIGURE 3-12 Configuring the IP address assignment in preparation for NLB.

MORE INFO **CONFIGURING NETWORK LOAD BALANCING**

See *http://technet.microsoft.com/library/hh831830* for more information on configuring NLB with Remote Access.

Configuring DirectAccess

You configure DirectAccess through the Remote Access Management Console. After the Getting Started Wizard is run the first time, you can change the settings for DirectAccess in this console by clicking the Edit button on any of the four main configuration areas:

- Client
- Remote Access Server
- Infrastructure Server
- Application Server

The changes are then applied to the configuration accordingly. For example, you can change the IP address assignment configuration from DHCP to a static pool of IPs within the Remote Access server configuration section. You can also set the compliance and support for down-level (Windows 7) computers in the Authentication pane of the Remote Access Setup Wizard as well, as shown in Figure 3-13.

FIGURE 3-13 The Authentication pane of the Remote Access Setup Wizard.

In the Infrastructure Server configuration, you can change settings such as the Network Location Server to use and other settings related to ancillary servers used in the Remote Access deployment.

> **MORE INFO   CONFIGURING DIRECTACCESS**
>
> See *http://technet.microsoft.com/library/hh831416* for more information on configuring DirectAccess.

THOUGHT EXPERIMENT
Deploying an end-to-end Remote Access solution

In the following thought experiment, apply what you've learned about this objective. You can find answers to these questions in the "Answers" section at the end of this chapter.

You are deploying an end-to-end Remote Access solution covering a partner site that needs VPN connectivity and supports Windows 7 and Windows 8 clients. In the data center, you have one server with a single network interface allocated to handle these connections, and supporting servers such as DNS and an Active Directory server already exist.

1. Describe the roles and features that you would likely install for this scenario.

2. Describe the high-level steps involved in deploying the solution with the roles and features that you installed.

Objective summary

- Remote Access includes numerous configuration wizards to assist in basic configuration for much of a DirectAccess and VPN configuration.
- The Site-to-Site VPN Wizard helps you create a site-to-site VPN configuration.
- Packet filters are configured within the Windows Firewall.
- Packet tracing enables you to provide an advanced level of logging for troubleshooting.
- Multisite Remote Access enables clients to connect to a different Remote Access server. This feature is configured with a wizard, and then entry points are added to the configuration.
- You can enable Network Load Balancing (NLB) in the Remote Access Management Console but must first add it as a Windows feature.

Objective review

Answer the following questions to test your knowledge of the information in this objective. You can find the answers to these questions and explanations of why each answer choice is correct or incorrect in the "Answers" section at the end of this chapter.

1. Which of the following aren't options for client access in a multisite deployment? (Choose two.)

    A. Assign Entry Points Automatically And Allow Clients To Select Manually

    B. Assign Entry Points Automatically Only

    C. Assign Entry Points Through DirectAccess Or Allow Clients To Select Manually

    D. Assign Entry Points Automatically Or Through DirectAccess

2. When configuring an NLB configuration, what do you first need to do?

    A. Enable the Network Load Balancing role.

    B. Enable the Network Load Balancing feature.

    C. Run the Network Load Balancing Wizard.

    D. Run the Enable Load Balancing Wizard.

3. Which type of packet tracing log overwrites any existing log file found in the same location?

    A. Existing

    B. Overwrite

    C. Circular

    D. Forward

Objective 3.4: Design a network protection solution

A common attack vector is through infected client computers that connect to corporate networks. The client computers are trusted within the network and therefore might have additional privileges that enable malware and viruses to propagate. Network Access Protection (NAP) and related technologies help lessen the chances of this type of attack.

EXAM TIP

For the exam, you should be familiar with NAP, including its concepts and how it assists with network protection. Within this objective are several links to additional information on NAP. If you're unfamiliar with NAP or need a refresher, you can follow the links to obtain additional background information on the technologies involved.

MORE INFO   **NETWORK ACCESS PROTECTION**

For background details on NAP, the information at *http://technet.microsoft.com/library/ hh831683.aspx* is helpful.

This objective covers the following topics:

■ Integrating DHCP, IPsec, VPN, and 802.1X

■ Planning for capacity and server placement

■ Planning for NPS and firewall access

Understanding network protection solutions

NAP ensures that computers connecting to the network through Remote Access have the required set of policies and are "healthy." Computers not found to be healthy have their communications limited. Designing a network protection solution involves deployment of NAP enforcement or several key areas including DHCP, IPsec, and VPN. This section examines considerations for the design of a network protection solution.

> **MORE INFO** **NAP OVERVIEW AND DESIGN GUIDE**
>
> See *http://technet.microsoft.com/library/cc754378* for an overview of NAP, including de-ployment considerations beyond those discussed here, and *http://technet.microsoft.com/library/dd125338.aspx* for a design guide for NAP.

DHCP

Integrating NAP with DHCP means that enforcement happens when a client attempts to obtain or renew a DHCP lease. This works only for IPv4 clients and only when they interact with the DHCP server to request an initial lease or to renew a lease. In other words, clients configured with static IP addresses won't ever interact with the DHCP server and, as a result, this enforcement method is ineffective.

Three components are involved in a NAP deployment for DHCP:

■ A DHCP NAP enforcement server

■ The NAP DHCP enforcement client with NAP-capable clients

■ A Network Policy Server (NPS)

NAP is enforced at the DHCP scope level and, as such, is configured in the DHCP manage-ment console. When configuring NAP on a server that isn't running the DHCP service, you need to install the Network Policy Server (NPS) role on the DHCP server and configure NPS to act as a Remote Authentication Dial-In User Service (RADIUS) proxy in order to forward con-nections to the local NPS server.

IPsec

IPsec enforcement can prevent non-compliant computers from communicating with compli-ant computers. With IPsec, you can set enforcement requirements for clients down to the individual IP address and/or port (TCP/UDP). This feature, coupled with the ability to restrict network communications to only compliant clients, makes IPsec enforcement the most robust NAP enforcement method available.

NAP with IPsec requires the following components:

- A health certificate server
- A Health Registration Authority (HRA)
- A Network Policy Server (NPS)
- The NAP IPsec enforcement client with NAP-capable clients

NAP with IPsec requires the HRA to have the NPS installed. The HRA NPS server is then configured as a RADIUS proxy to forward connections to the local NPS server.

VPN

VPN enforcement means that health policies are enforced when a client connects to the VPN. This requires the Remote Access role, and the NPS must be configured as the primary RADIUS server. The VPN servers also must be configured as RADIUS clients.

VPN enforcement has two components:

- A VPN enforcement server
- NAP-capable clients running the NAP Remote Access and Extensible Authentication Protocol (EAP) enforcement clients

A special Allow Full Network Access For A Limited Time option enables clients to connect to the network for a certain time period after which they are disconnected, regardless of compliance level. On reconnection, non-compliant computers are restricted.

802.1X

802.1X compliance enforcement enables the NPS to work with the 802.1X network component to keep non-compliant clients in a restricted network.

NAP for 802.1X uses the following components:

- 802.1X networking components such as wireless access points or switches
- NAP-capable clients with the NAP service and EAP enforcement client

Planning for capacity and server placement

When considering capacity planning for a network policy deployment, you need to consider how to use each server and for which roles each server will be responsible. In other words, if one server is responsible for multiple roles, its performance is affected accordingly. The location of servers or the topology of the network also affects the capacity-planning decision, as does the availability requirement within the organization.

The servers involved in a network policy deployment each have their own capacity considerations.

NAP enforcement server

NAP enforcement servers include those that provide access to network resources such as VPN servers and DHCP servers as well as Health Registration Authority (HRA) servers. These servers might have cryptographic requirements that negatively affect their performance.

Table 3-5 lists considerations for when examining the capacity for the NAP enforcement server.

> **NOTE** **ENFORCEMENT SERVER**
>
> A server dedicated to the HRA role can support at least 20 requests per second. The enforcement server role is typically installed with other network access services such as a VPN, DHCP, or IPsec server.

TABLE 3-5 Capacity considerations for the NAP enforcement server

Consideration	Description
Statement of Health (SoH) Validity Period	NAP clients renew their access more frequently with a shorter SoH validity period. By default, clients attempt to renew their certificates 15 minutes before expiration.
Roles on Server	If the server is responsible for other NPS roles or other services, its capacity to serve as a NAP enforcement server is affected.
Network access profile	The enforcement server's ability to service requests is affected by the number of simultaneous requests, such as during peak times.
Group Policy updates	When clients receive Group Policy updates in an IPsec enforcement scenario, each client attempts to renew its access, thereby affecting performance and capacity.

> **MORE INFO** **CAPACITY PLANNING AND PLACEMENT**
>
> See *http://technet.microsoft.com/library/dd125359* for more information on capacity planning for the NAP enforcement server and *http://technet.microsoft.com/library/dd125384* for information on placement.

Health policy server

The health policy server provides authentication, including the health status of the client computer. The health policy server does this through the NPS RADIUS service, which can service a large number of requests without much impact to performance. NPS can also be load balanced through a RADIUS server group.

Central to a NAP deployment, the health policy server needs to communicate not only with clients but also with several other servers involved in the NAP deployment. The criteria for deploying more than one health policy server are as follows:

- Load balancing and failover
- Local health evaluation, such as at a remote site
- Co-location with multiple domain controllers

> **MORE INFO** **HEALTH POLICY SERVER**
>
> See *http://technet.microsoft.com/library/dd125385* for more information on capacity planning for the health policy server and *http://technet.microsoft.com/library/dd125325* for more information on placement.

NAP certificate authority servers

The HRA role uses a certificate authority (CA) in the organization. Multiple CAs can be used, and the HRA server attempts to contact each in a round-robin fashion until one responds. The CA used for HRA should be dedicated to issuing health certificates; otherwise, performance can be negatively affected. A standalone CA can have slightly higher performance than an enterprise CA for issuing health certificates.

NAP CA servers are used when you deploy a full IPsec enforcement or a no-enforcement implementation.

> **MORE INFO** **CERTIFICATE AUTHORITY SERVERS**
>
> See *http://technet.microsoft.com/library/dd125318* for more information on capacity planning for CAs and *http://technet.microsoft.com/library/dd125388* for information on placement.

Remediation and health requirement servers

A NAP remediation server helps non-compliant computers become compliant by providing software updates and anti-virus services. A health requirement server works with the health policy server to establish requirements for System Health Validators (SHVs). SHVs ensure that the firewall is enabled, check to make sure that certain updates are applied, check how long since updates have been obtained, and so on. Numerous third-party SHVs are available.

Because remediation and health requirement servers are optional and the services offered depend on your deployment, no specific guidance is available for capacity planning their design. A mitigating factor in the design is that the servers shouldn't be used heavily, assuming that clients are typically compliant.

When placing remediation servers on the network, you should keep them separate from the main corporate network because the clients using them will be non-compliant, will violate at least one policy, and can be infected with malware.

Health requirement servers need to communicate with the health policy server which dictates their placement within the NAP deployment.

> **MORE INFO** **REMEDIATION SERVERS, HEALTH REQUIREMENT SERVERS, AND NPSS**
>
> See *http://technet.microsoft.com/library/dd125378* for more information on remediation servers and *http://technet.microsoft.com/library/dd125316* for information on health requirement servers. See *http://technet.microsoft.com/library/cc732912* for more information on Network Policy Servers.

Planning for NPS and firewall access

You need to consider several requirements when designing firewall access and an NPS solution. The firewall considerations typically need to be addressed both on the servers participating as well as any intermediate network-level firewalls in between those servers and between the servers and the clients.

> **MORE INFO** **FIREWALL REQUIREMENTS**
>
> See *http://technet.microsoft.com/library/cc732902* for more information on the firewall requirements involved in a network protection design.

Because RADIUS traffic uses UDP ports 1812, 1813, 1645, and 1646, this traffic must be allowed to access servers involved in this traffic, such as the NPS server. When installed, this traffic is automatically added as an exception on the NPS server.

The NPS server serves as a management interface to the RADIUS server, RADIUS proxy, and NAP policy server. You can configure NPS in several complex scenarios: as a full RADIUS server implementation, as a proxy to another RADIUS server, as both a RADIUS server and proxy, as a RADIUS server with remote accounting servers, and as a remote RADIUS to Windows User Mapping server. This last scenario means that the NPS server forwards the authentication request to a remote RADIUS server but performs authorization with Windows user account information.

> **MORE INFO** **NETWORK POLICY SERVER**
>
> See *http://technet.microsoft.com/library/cc771347* for more information on the Network Policy Server.

Remediation Network

As previously discussed, remediation servers provide services to clients that are non-compliant for any number of reasons including virus infections or lack of updates. The remediation network should be logically separate from the corporate network so as to lessen the chance that an infected computer can impact network performance and reliability. The remediation network should include those services that can assist the client in becoming compliant, including antivirus signature servers, Windows update servers, domain controllers, DHCP servers, DNS servers, and other infrastructure services necessary to enable the client to become compliant.

THOUGHT EXPERIMENT
Using protection in an NPS solution

In the following thought experiment, apply what you've learned about this objective. You can find answers to these questions in the "Answers" section at the end of this chapter.

You're deploying a network protection solution and need to use the protection on DHCP and incorporate a DirectAccess IPsec solution.

1. Describe the NPS-related services that you'll need to deploy.

2. Describe the pitfalls of the DHCP method as it relates to overall network protection.

Objective summary

- Designing a network protection solution involves deployment of several components.
- Microsoft offers protection solutions at the DHCP server through IPsec, VPN, and 802.1X.
- IPsec provides the strongest level of protection.
- When using DHCP for protection, clients can circumvent the protection and gain access to the network with a static IP or other addressing.
- Microsoft identifies considerations for capacity planning of the various components in an NPS solution.
- When designing firewalling for NPS, you should include not only the local Windows firewall on the servers involved in the solution, but also any intermediate firewalls.
- The remediation network should be separate from the corporate network and should include resources such that the client can become compliant.

Objective review

Answer the following questions to test your knowledge of the information in this objective. You can find the answers to these questions and explanations of why each answer choice is correct or incorrect in the "Answers" section at the end of this chapter.

1. When working with firewalls in an NPS environment, which ports do you need to open for RADIUS?

   A. UDP: 1645, 1646, 1812, 1813

   B. TCP: 1645, 1646, 1812, 1813

   C. UDP: 1645 and 1812 and TCP 1646 and 1813

   D. UDP and TCP: 1645, 1646, 1812, 1813

2. When deploying the NAP enforcement server, a _____ validity period for clients results in _____ load on the server. (Choose all correct answers.)

   A. shorter, less

   B. shorter, more

   C. longer, more

   D. longer, less

3. Which of the following is *not* a reason for deploying more than one health policy server?

   A. For load balancing and failover

   B. For local health evaluation such as at a remote site

   C. For deployment to an SHV implementation

   D. For co-location with multiple domain controllers

Objective 3.5: Implement a network protection solution

Network protection is more important than ever. The sheer volume of automated threats means that automated protection and remediation is valuable and necessary in an organization. This objective examines the network protection solutions available, including those available with Windows Server 2012 as well as those available through System Center Configuration Manager 2012.

This objective covers the following topics:

- Implementing multiple RADIUS servers
- Configuring NAP enforcement for IPsec and 802.1X
- Deploying and configuring the Endpoint Protection Client
- Creating antimalware and firewall policies
- Monitoring for compliance

Implementing multiple RADIUS servers

A RADIUS server group takes advantage of the load-balancing capabilities of NPS and can be used to provide redundancy. You can configure RADIUS server groups within the Network Policy Server management console by selecting New from the Remote RADIUS Server Groups context menu.

Creating a new RADIUS server group invokes the New Remote RADIUS Server Group dialog box, as shown in Figure 3-14.

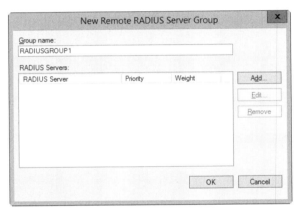

FIGURE 3-14 Adding a new remote RADIUS server group.

When you're presented with the dialog box in Figure 3-14, you enter the group name and click Add to add RADIUS servers. This presents the Add RADIUS Server dialog box shown in Figure 3-15.

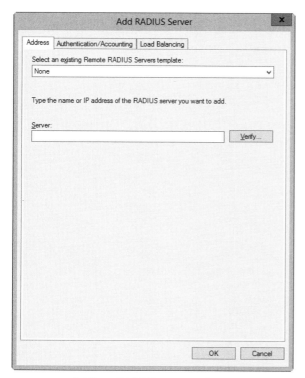

FIGURE 3-15 Adding a RADIUS server to the server group.

The Authentication/Accounting tab, shown in Figure 3-16, enables you to set such things as the shared secret and port to use for authentication and accounting requests.

FIGURE 3-16 The Authentication/Accounting tab contains items related to the actual authentication and accounting requests for RADIUS.

The Load Balancing tab, shown in Figure 3-17, enables you to set priority and overall behavior for sharing the load among the servers. For example, setting a priority of 1 for multiple servers enables those servers to share load, but if you have a server that's busier than others, its priority can be lowered accordingly so that it receives fewer RADIUS requests. Alternately, if servers share the same priority, the Weight value can be used to determine the load-sharing behavior.

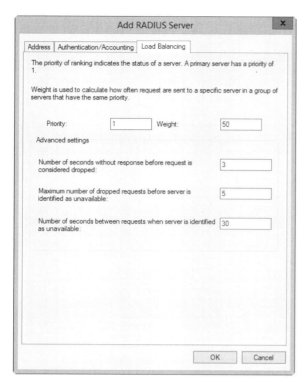

FIGURE 3-17 The Load Balancing configuration for a RADIUS server group.

MORE INFO **CONFIGURING REMOTE RADIUS SERVER GROUPS**

See *http://technet.microsoft.com/library/dd296908* for more information on configuring remote RADIUS server groups.

Configuring NAP enforcement for IPsec and 802.1X

NAP configuration for IPsec and 802.1X means that clients interacting through those methods are subject to the NPS policies and health validation. Configuration of both IPsec and 802.1X NAP enforcement policies is accomplished within the Network Policy Server management console, under the NPS (Local) details pane, as shown in Figure 3-18.

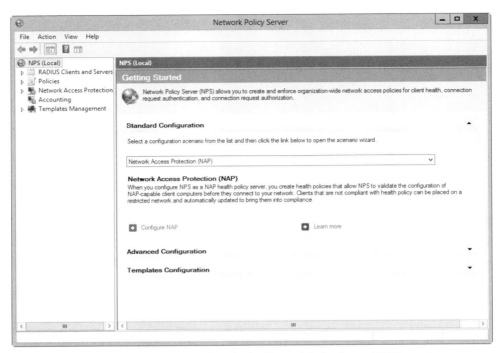

FIGURE 3-18 Configuring enforcement policies in the Network Policy Server MMC snap-in.

IPsec policy enforcement

Within the Standard Configuration section, selecting Configure NAP invokes the Configure NAP Wizard.

In the first dialog box of this wizard, shown in Figure 3-19, you choose IPsec With Health Registration Authority (HRA) from the drop-down.

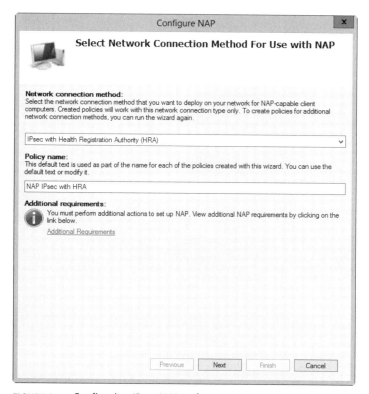

FIGURE 3-19 Configuring IPsec NAP enforcement.

The Specify NAP Enforcement Servers Running HRA dialog box is next (see Figure 3-20).

RADIUS clients are network access servers, not client computers. If the local computer is running HRA, you can skip this step and click Next.

If you want to add remote HRA servers as RADIUS clients, click Add. All remote HRA servers that you add must also run NPS. Also, remote HRA-NPS servers must forward connection requests to this NPS server (the local computer).

FIGURE 3-20 Specifying the server for HRA.

If you need a RADIUS client, you can specify it on this dialog box by clicking Add, which reveals the New RADIUS Client dialog box shown in Figure 3-21.

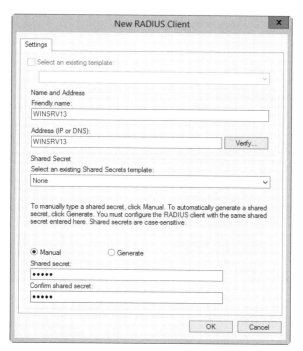

FIGURE 3-21 Adding a new RADIUS client.

However, if the local server is also an HRA, adding a new client isn't necessary, and you can just click Next in the Specify NAP Enforcement Servers Running HRA dialog box (refer to Figure 3-20). Doing so opens the Configure Machine Groups dialog box, as shown in Figure 3-22.

FIGURE 3-22 The Configure Machine Groups dialog box is optional.

If the policy will apply only to certain client computers, they can be added here through an Active Directory group; otherwise, the policy will apply to all users. Clicking Next reveals the Define NAP Health Policy dialog box, shown in Figure 3-23.

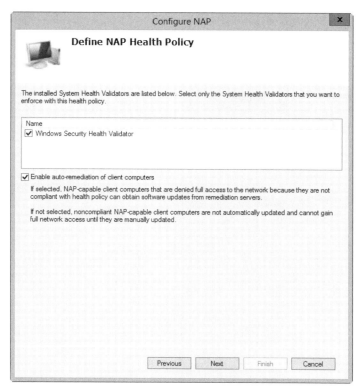

FIGURE 3-23 Configuring the SHVs to apply for this policy.

In this dialog box, you choose the Security Health Validators (SHVs) that you want to apply for this policy and whether you want computers affected by the policy to be automatically remediated. Clicking Next reveals a confirmation dialog box in which you click Finish.

> **MORE INFO   CONFIGURING IPSEC AND NAP**
>
> See *http://technet.microsoft.com/library/dd314154* for more information on configuring IPsec and NAP.

802.1X policy enforcement

802.1X policy enforcement comes in two varieties: wired and wireless. In a wired scenario, the access requests come from switches; in a wireless scenario, the access requests come from wireless access points. Each policy is configured separately.

The policies begin their configuration in the same Configure NAP Wizard seen earlier in Figure 3-19, except this time, rather than select IPsec, you select IEEE 802.1X (Wired) or IEEE 802.1X (Wireless), depending on the type of access devices used.

If you choose the wired scenario, the next dialog box you'll see is the Specify 802.1X Authenticating Switches dialog box shown in Figure 3-24.

FIGURE 3-24 Specifying 802.1X switches for a wired deployment.

If you chose a wireless scenario, you'll use the dialog box in Figure 3-25 to choose authenticating switches or access points.

FIGURE 3-25 Choosing the authenticating switches or access points in a wireless deployment of 802.1X.

Unlike an IPsec deployment, RADIUS clients need to be configured for the 802.1X scenario but can be added later. Refer to Figure 3-21 for an example of the New RADIUS Client dialog box.

With 802.1X, you can also specify user groups as well as machine groups, and this is shown on the Configure User Groups and Machine Groups dialog box (see Figure 3-26).

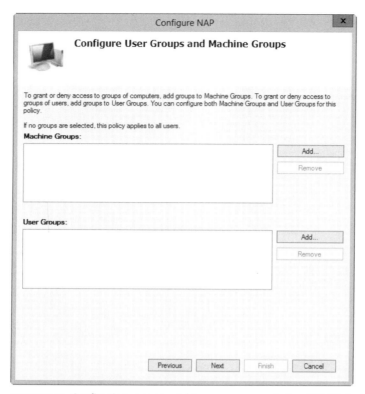

FIGURE 3-26 Configuring user or machine groups as part of an 802.1X deployment.

Next, you configure an authentication method, as shown in Figure 3-27.

FIGURE 3-27 Configuring an authentication method as part of an 802.1X deployment.

You can configure traffic controls through RADIUS attributes or VLANs on the next dialog box (see Figure 3-28).

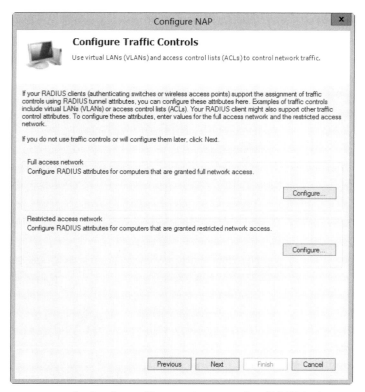

FIGURE 3-28 Configuring traffic controls as part of an 802.1X deployment.

Finally, you configure the health policy, including the SHVs and remediation policy (see Figure 3-29). You also can configure the handling of clients that can't deploy NAP in this dialog box.

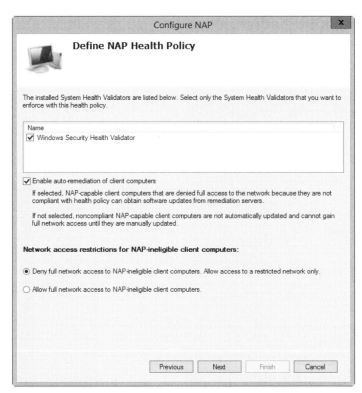

FIGURE 3-29 Defining the SHVs to be applied to this policy along with how to handle computers that aren't NAP-capable.

MORE INFO   **CONFIGURING 802.1X**

See *http://technet.microsoft.com/library/dd314181* for more information on configuring 802.1X enforcement.

Deploying and configuring the Endpoint Protection Client

The Endpoint Protection Client is deployed as part of System Center Configuration Manager. Deployment of the Endpoint Protection Client assumes that you have Configuration Manager already installed in your environment. The following steps need to be followed to configure and deploy Endpoint Protection Client.

Create Endpoint Protection Site System role

The Site System role, which must be deployed at the top of the hierarchy on a central administration or standalone primary site, needs to be installed first. In the Administration workspace of the System Center 2012 console, select Servers And Site Settings from the Site Configuration node and then choose Add Site System Roles from the context menu for the server on which Endpoint Protection is to be deployed.

Doing so launches the Add Site System Roles Wizard, as shown in Figure 3-30.

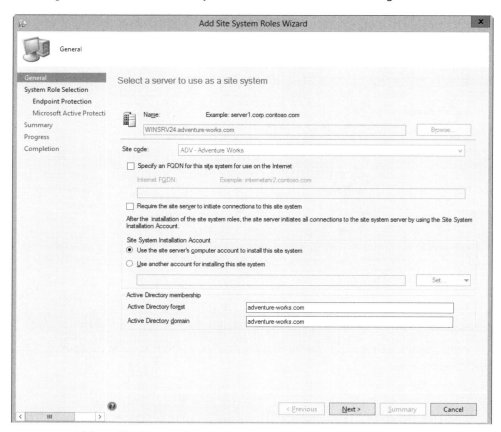

FIGURE 3-30 Adding a Site System role.

Following this wizard, you next choose the Site System role to apply. When choosing the Endpoint Protection role you might receive a warning, like the one shown in Figure 3-31.

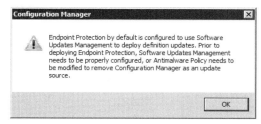

FIGURE 3-31 A warning to change policy to configure Software Updates Management or to remove Configuration Manager as an update source.

Dismissing the warning reveals the System Role Selection pane shown in Figure 3-32.

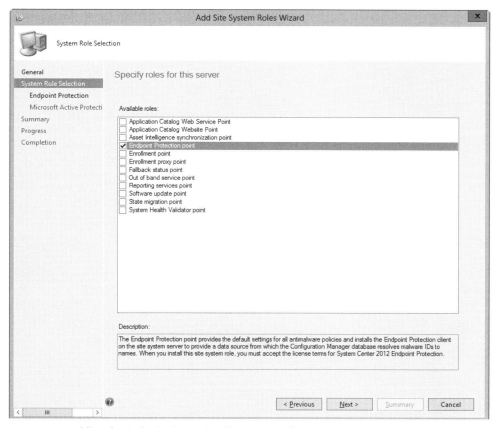

FIGURE 3-32 Adding the Endpoint Protection Site System role.

Configure alerts

You configure alerts to notify when specific events occur. You can configure alerts for End-point Protection in the Assets and Compliance workspace within the Device Collections node. In the Device Collections node, shown in Figure 3-33, selecting Properties from the collection to which the alerts should be deployed reveals the properties for that collection.

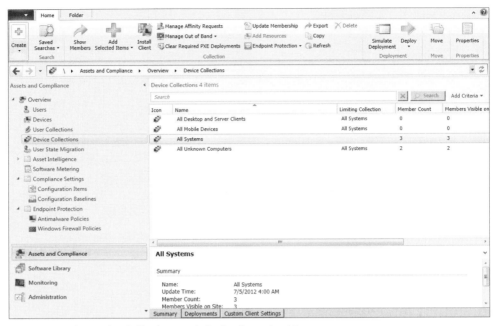

FIGURE 3-33 The Device Collections node in Configuration Manager.

Use the Alerts tab within the collection's Properties sheet to add alerts. Several criteria are available, as shown in Figure 3-34.

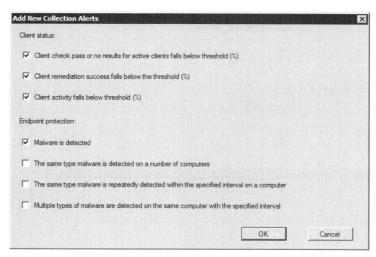

FIGURE 3-34 Add alerts for a collection.

After you click OK, the Alerts tab shows the selected alerts (see Figure 3-35).

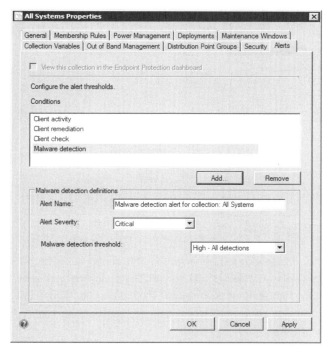

FIGURE 3-35 Configuring alerts for a collection.

Configure the default antimalware policy

The next step in configuring Endpoint Protection is to configure the default antimalware policy. This topic is discussed in the next section.

Configure custom client settings

After the default antimalware policy is configured, you next need to configure custom settings for the client. In the Client Settings node of the Administration workspace, click Create Custom Client Device Settings. Doing so reveals a dialog box like the one in Figure 3-36.

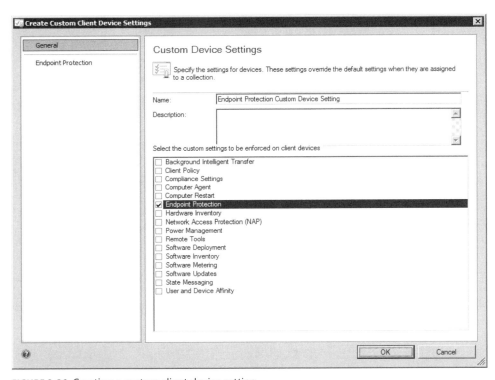

FIGURE 3-36 Creating a custom client device setting.

An important piece of configuration that needs to happen within this dialog box is found in the Endpoint Protection pane, as shown in Figure 3-37. By default, the policy isn't set to be managed and installed, so you need to change Manage Endpoint Protection Client On Client Computers to True.

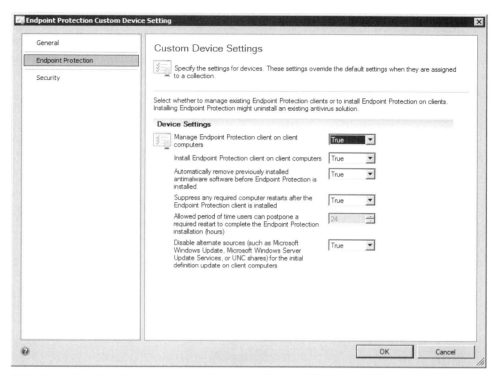

FIGURE 3-37 Changing Manage Endpoint Protection Client On Client Computers to True.

Deploying a policy

You deploy a policy after creating a custom policy; the default antimalware policy cannot be deployed. To deploy a policy, choose Deploy from the Home tab of the Endpoint Protection node in the Assets and Compliance workspace. When you click Deploy for the policy to be deployed, you're prompted to select the collection to which the policy will be deployed.

Setting up antimalware and firewall policies

Endpoint Protection offers two types of policies: Antimalware and Windows Firewall. Settings for custom policies are inherited from a default Antimalware policy. Because no default Windows Firewall policy exists, a custom one needs to be created.

EXAM TIP

A custom Antimalware policy overrides the default policy.

Creating an antimalware policy

You create an antimalware policy in Configuration Manager within the Assets and Compliance workspace in the Endpoint Protection node. Click Create Antimalware Policy in the Antimalware Policies area. Several predefined templates are included and can be used as a basis for creating a custom policy. The templates are found in the AdminConsole\XMLStorage\ EPTemplates folder within the Configuration Manager installation folder. Creating a template launches the wizard shown in Figure 3-38.

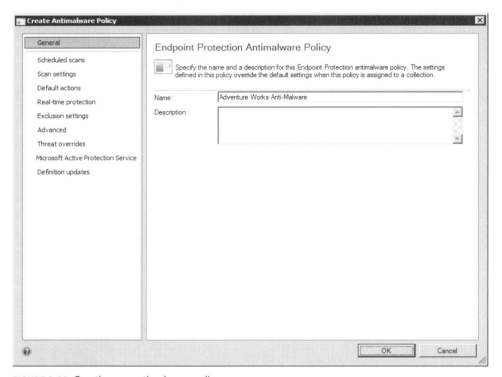

FIGURE 3-38 Creating an antimalware policy.

The settings for the policy are inherited from the Default Client Antimalware Policy at the time of creation. In other words, if you make a change to Default Client Antimalware Policy, that change isn't propagated to existing custom policies.

Each pane of the Create Antimalware Policy Wizard contains the settings relevant to that pane. For example, the Scan Settings pane contains information about what to scan, but the Real-Time Protection pane also contains additional information about scanning. Figures 3-39 and 3-40 show examples of each of these panes.

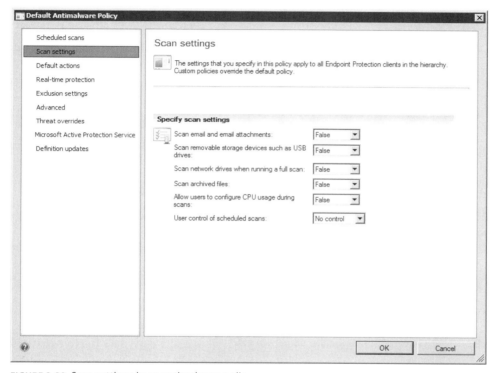

FIGURE 3-39 Scan settings in an antimalware policy.

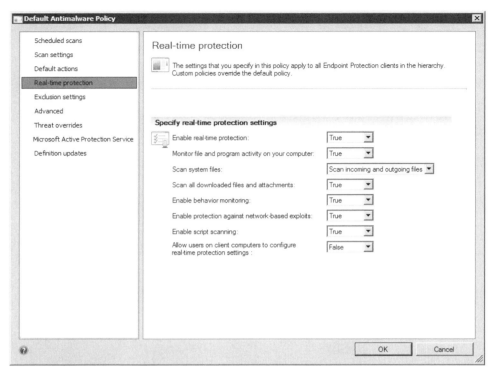

FIGURE 3-40 Real-time protection settings in an antimalware policy.

MORE INFO **ANTIMALWARE AND HEALTH POLICIES**

See *http://technet.microsoft.com/en-us/library/hh508785* for information on creating antimalware policies in Configuration Manager. See *http://technet.microsoft.com/library/dd314173* for information on health policies in NAP.

Creating Windows Firewall Policy

You can create a Windows Firewall policy in Configuration Manager within the Assets and Compliance workspace in the Endpoint Protection node. Click Create Windows Firewall Policy in the Windows Firewall Policies area to launch the Create Windows Firewall Policy Wizard. The first pane of this wizard is where you set the name and description for the policy; you configure the policy on the next pane, as shown in Figure 3-41.

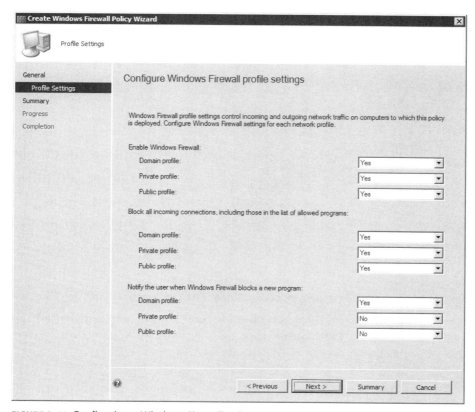

FIGURE 3-41 Configuring a Windows Firewall policy.

By default, the Enable Windows Firewall select box is set to Not Configured for the Domain, Private, and Public profiles. Choosing Yes to enable the profile enables the corresponding Block and Notify behaviors to be set.

Like with the Antimalware policy, you deploy the Windows Firewall policy after it's created by selecting Deploy from the Home tab. Deployment of the policy can take several hours in certain scenarios, to reduce possible network issues. The Deploy Windows Firewall Policy dialog box, opened when you click Deploy, enables the policy to be set on a schedule in addition to the choice of collection. Figure 3-42 shows this dialog box.

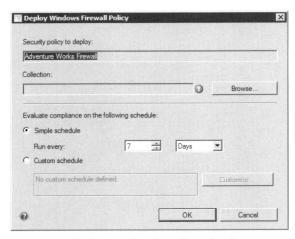

FIGURE 3-42 Deploying a Windows Firewall policy.

> **MORE INFO**   **DEPLOYING WINDOWS FIREWALL POLICIES AND IP FILTERS**
>
> See *http://technet.microsoft.com/library/hh508765* for more information on deploying a
> Windows Firewall Policy with Endpoint Protection and *http://technet.microsoft.com/library/
> dd314145* for information on deploying IP filters with NAP.

Monitoring compliance

You can monitor compliance with Endpoint Protection in the Monitoring workspace. The
Client Status node and the System Center 2012 Endpoint Protection Status node contain
information about events related to client compliance.

Figure 3-43 shows the Endpoint Protection Monitoring view.

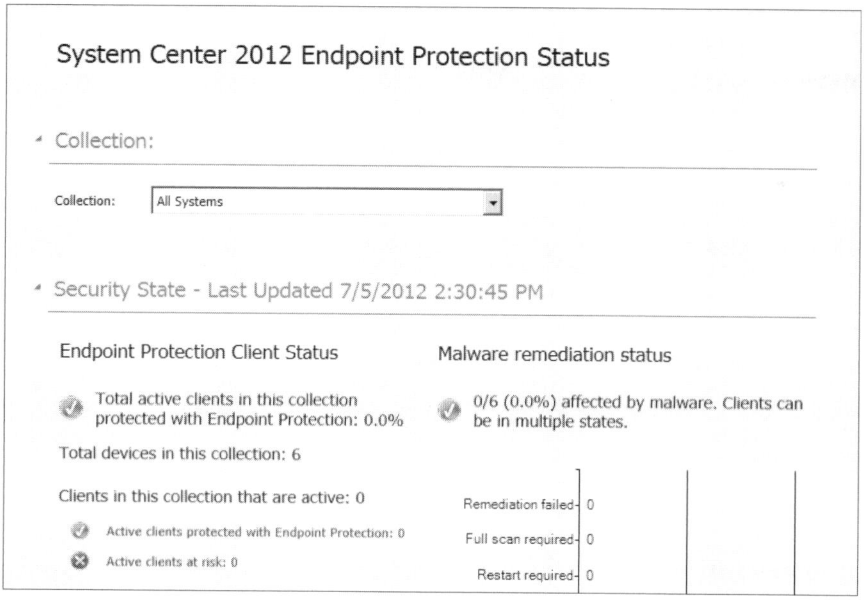

System Center 2012 Endpoint Protection Status

Collection:

Collection: All Systems

Security State - Last Updated 7/5/2012 2:30:45 PM

Endpoint Protection Client Status

Total active clients in this collection protected with Endpoint Protection: 0.0%

Total devices in this collection: 6

Clients in this collection that are active: 0

Active clients protected with Endpoint Protection: 0

Active clients at risk: 0

Malware remediation status

0/6 (0.0%) affected by malware. Clients can be in multiple states.

Remediation failed- 0

Full scan required- 0

Restart required- 0

FIGURE 3-43 Endpoint Protection Status monitoring in Configuration Manager.

Compliance-related settings are set in the Assets and Compliance workspace within Configuration Manager. In this workspace, the Compliance Settings node enables both Configuration Items and Configuration Baselines to be created.

MORE INFO   **COMPLIANCE SETTINGS**

See *http://technet.microsoft.com/en-us/library/gg681958* for more information on compliance settings in Configuration Manager.

THOUGHT EXPERIMENT
Implementing Endpoint Protection

In the following thought experiment, apply what you've learned about this objective. You can find answers to these questions in the "Answers" section at the end of this chapter.

You're tasked with creating an Endpoint Protection implementation. Configuration Manager is installed and its initial configuration performed on a domain member computer, and the domain controller is available. The Configuration Manager client has already been installed on several hundred computers as well.

1. Describe the steps necessary to deploy Endpoint Protection on the server.

2. Describe any additional steps necessary to deploy an antimalware policy.

Objective summary

- A RADIUS server group enables load balancing and redundancy in a Network Access Protection scenario.
- NAP policy enforcement is configured based on the access method, such as IPsec and 802.1X.
- The Endpoint Protection Client, part of System Center 2012 Configuration Manager, enables advanced antimalware and firewall policy management as well as malware remediation.
- The Endpoint Protection Client is deployed as a Site System role.
- Deploying Endpoint Protection requires that you create a custom Antimalware policy.
- Custom antimalware and Windows Firewall policies are created in the Assets and Compliance workspace.
- Configuration Manager has powerful monitoring capabilities for determining client compliance. These are accessed in the Monitoring workspace.

Objective review

Answer the following questions to test your knowledge of the information in this objective. You can find the answers to these questions and explanations of why each answer choice is correct or incorrect in the "Answers" section at the end of this chapter.

1. When two servers in a RADIUS server group have the same priority, which setting is used to determine how often requests are sent to each server?

    A. Primary

    B. Rotation

    C. Weight

    D. Filter

2. Deploying an 802.1X access protection method requires which of the following?

    A. 802.1X-capable network hardware

    B. Active Firewall Rules

    C. Designated 802.1X Actions

    D. Firewall Policy Creation

3. Which type of NAP enforcement requires an authentication method to be defined?

    A. RADIUS

    B. Group Policy

    C. Firewall

    D. 802.1X

Chapter summary

- Designing a VPN solution with Windows Server 2012 involves creation of an architecture for remote access.
- You can use various tools to assist with network protection.
- DirectAccess provides an advanced remote access solution.
- Implementing network protection occurs at various levels.
- DirectAccess comes with three scenarios: end-to-end, selected server, and full intranet access.

Answers

This section contains the solutions to the thought experiments and answers to the objective review questions in this chapter.

Objective 3.1: Thought experiment

You should set up an enterprise CA and use group policy–based auto enrollment to ensure that all domain members receive the certificate from an enterprise CA. The certificate needs to have client authentication Extended Key Usage (EKU). Finally, the certificate configured in the DirectAccess configuration should be the same used by the clients and servers.

Objective 3.1: Review

1. **Correct answer:** C

    A. **Incorrect:** Although the port is correct, the protocol (TCP) isn't correct for this answer.

    B. **Incorrect:** TCP/62000 isn't used for a Teredo solution.

    C. **Correct:** UDP/3544 must be allowed inbound and outbound for Teredo on IPv4.

    D. **Incorrect:** TCP/443 is used for HTTPS.

2. **Correct answer:** B

    A. **Incorrect:** IP-HTTPS is a scenario that needs certificates.

    B. **Correct:** PPTP wasn't listed as one of the scenarios for certificate design considerations.

    C. **Incorrect:** IPsec uses certificates.

    D. **Incorrect:** Network location server uses certificates.

3. **Correct answer:** A

    A. **Correct:** The Server Authentication object identifier is used in the EKU field.

    B. **Incorrect:** The common name isn't used in the EKU field.

    C. **Incorrect:** The Server Name OID isn't used for this field.

    D. **Incorrect:** The IP address of the Remote Access server isn't used for this field.

Objective 3.2: Thought experiment

1. You would likely perform an offline migration because all other clients and servers involved will already be running Windows Server 2012. Therefore, performing a side-by-side migration isn't necessary.

2. The DirectAccess scenario is an end-to-end deployment. You would choose this because the entire infrastructure can use the advanced features of Windows Server 2012 DirectAccess.

Objective 3.2: Review

1. **Correct answer:** A

   A. **Correct:** Infrastructure deployment is where you deploy service and role servers that are used with the DirectAccess deployment, aside from the actual Direct-Access server and the application servers.

   B. **Incorrect:** Application servers represent the actual applications and tools that the clients will use.

   C. **Incorrect:** Client configuration deployment isn't a step.

   D. **Incorrect:** DNS server deployment isn't a step.

2. **Correct answer:** C

   A. **Incorrect:** An offline migration causes downtime when the existing server is taken offline to bring up the new server.

   B. **Incorrect:** Intraserver isn't a real migration type.

   C. **Correct:** Side-by-side migration brings both servers up at the same time using different network information, thus enabling clients to connect to the new server and old server as needed.

   D. **Incorrect:** End-to-end isn't a migration scenario.

3. **Correct answer:** B

   A. **Incorrect:** DirectAccess requires one network interface in Windows Server 2012.

   B. **Correct:** DirectAccess can now be deployed behind NAT and thus needs only one interface.

   C. **Incorrect:** DirectAccess doesn't require three interfaces.

   D. **Incorrect:** DirectAccess doesn't require six interfaces.

Objective 3.3: Thought experiment

1. For this scenario, you would install the Remote Access role with the DirectAccess and VPN (not routing) subrole. You don't need any additional features because the deployment involves only one server; otherwise, you might be tempted to install the Network Load Balancing feature.

2. Overall, you'll need to walk through the Getting Started Wizard and deploy both DirectAccess and VPN. You should set up the Remote Access solution to support both Windows 7 and Windows 8 clients on the Authentication page of the Remote Access Setup Wizard.

Objective 3.3: Review

1. **Correct answers:** C and D
   A. **Incorrect:** Assign Entry Points Automatically And Allow Clients To Select Manually is an option.
   B. **Incorrect:** Assign Entry Points Automatically Only is an option.
   C. **Correct:** Assign Entry Points Through Directaccess Or Allow Clients To Select Manually isn't an option.
   D. **Correct:** Assign Entry Points Automatically Or Through DirectAccess isn't an option.

2. **Correct answer:** B
   A. **Incorrect:** Network Load Balancing is a feature, not a role.
   B. **Correct:** You must first enable the Network Load Balancing feature before attempting to configure NLB Remote Access.
   C. **Incorrect:** This isn't a valid option.
   D. **Incorrect:** The Enable Load Balancing Wizard must be executed after the feature is installed.

3. **Correct answer:** C
   A. **Incorrect:** This option appends to an existing log.
   B. **Incorrect:** Overwrite isn't a valid option.
   C. **Correct:** Circular overwrites the log file.
   D. **Incorrect:** Forward isn't a valid option.

Objective 3.4: Thought experiment

1. For IPsec, you'll need a health certificate server, a Health Registration Authority (HRA), requisite CAs, a network policy server, and clients that can run the IPsec enforcement client. DHCP requires the DHCP enforcement server, the network policy server, and clients capable of NAP.

2. With DHCP, a client can circumvent or will not be part of the solution if it uses a static IP address or doesn't renew its lease.

Objective 3.4: Review

1. **Correct answer:** A

    A. **Correct:** UDP: 1645, 1646, 1812, and 1813 are the ports and protocol involved in RADIUS.

    B. **Incorrect:** The ports were correct but the protocol, TCP, was not. RADIUS uses UDP.

    C. **Incorrect:** RADIUS doesn't use TCP.

    D. **Incorrect:** RADIUS doesn't use TCP.

2. **Correct answers:** B and D

    A. **Incorrect:** A shorter validity period means more load on the server because clients need to renew more frequently.

    B. **Correct:** A shorter validity period means more load on the server because clients need to renew more frequently.

    C. **Incorrect:** A longer validity period means less load on the server because clients don't need to renew as often.

    D. **Correct:** A longer validity period means less load on the server because clients don't need to renew as often.

3. **Correct answer:** C

    A. **Incorrect:** Load balancing and failover is a valid reason.

    B. **Incorrect:** Local health evaluation such as at a remote site is a valid reason.

    C. **Correct:** For deployment to an SHV, implementation isn't a valid reason.

    D. **Incorrect:** Co-location with multiple domain controllers is a valid reason.

Objective 3.5: Thought experiment

1. Deploying the server side of Endpoint Protection involves several steps. First, you need to enable the Site System role for Endpoint Protection on the server. Second, you need to configure alerts. Then, create an antimalware policy, and finally, configure custom client settings.

2. After you create an antimalware policy, you can deploy it by selecting Deploy from within Configuration Manager.

Objective 3.5: Review

1. **Correct answer:** C

   A. **Incorrect:** Primary isn't an option.

   B. **Incorrect:** Rotation isn't an option.

   C. **Correct:** Weight determines how often requests are sent to servers with the same priority.

   D. **Incorrect:** Filter isn't an option.

2. **Correct answer:** A

   A. **Correct:** 802.1X-capable network hardware is required for deploying 802.1X.

   B. **Incorrect:** Active Firewall Rules isn't an option.

   C. **Incorrect:** Designated 802.1X Actions isn't an available option.

   D. **Incorrect:** Firewall Policy Creation doesn't relate to the access protection mechanism.

3. **Correct answer:** D

   A. **Incorrect:** RADIUS isn't a NAP enforcement method.

   B. **Incorrect:** Group Policy isn't a NAP enforcement method.

   C. **Incorrect:** Firewall isn't a NAP enforcement method.

   D. **Correct:** 802.1X requires setting of an authentication method such as PEAP.

CHAPTER 4

Design and implement an Active Directory infrastructure (logical)

This chapter looks at Active Directory, primarily from a design standpoint, with a bit of implementation thrown in around forest and domain deployment. Included in this chapter are items such as the overall forest and domain design, Group Policy design, and design of an Active Directory permission model.

Objectives in this chapter:

- Objective 4-1: Design a forest and domain infrastructure
- Objective 4-2: Implement a forest and domain infrastructure
- Objective 4-3: Design a Group Policy strategy
- Objective 4-4: Design an Active Directory permission model

Objective 4.1: Design a forest and domain infrastructure

Designing an Active Directory Domain Services (AD DS) design is a complex but important process because it defines and reflects the organization's security and operations. Taking time to design a proper forest and domain infrastructure is important. Understanding the concepts that go into this design is what this first objective is all about. This objective examines some of the considerations previously identified.

This objective covers the following topics:

- Design considerations, including multi-forest architecture, trusts, functional levels, domain upgrade, domain migration, forest restructure, and Hybrid Cloud services

Multi-forest architecture

You might choose a multi-forest architecture for several reasons, including organizational,
operational, or regulatory requirements. For example, part of an organization may need to
implement certain constraints on the security of the forest that don't apply to all areas of the
organization.

An important concept in forest design is the scope of authority for the service administrator. By participating in an Active Directory forest, the forest owner and thereby the service
administrators have control of and access to all data within the forest.

The logical structure of Active Directory enables you to have either autonomy or isolation.
An autonomous structure has control of resources, but others at a higher level may also have
control. Two types of autonomy exist: service and data.

Service autonomy means that individual control is exerted over service management, in
whole or in part. Data autonomy means control over the data in the directory, in whole or in
part, although it can also mean control over all or part of member computers.

An isolation scenario grants exclusive control over a resource, with no higher-power
authorities involved in the resource's management. Like with the autonomy scenario, you can
use isolation for both service and data isolation. Service isolation means that no other authority or administrators have control over services, whereas data isolation means that no other
authority or administrators can control or even view data in the directory, including member
computers.

Choosing the logical structure is an important step in designing an Active Directory solution and dictates whether the design will include multiple forests. For example, in a scenario
requiring isolation, multiple forests will be needed because that's the only way to limit control
over AD DS resources.

Table 4-1 lists the three forest design models. An organization will likely use a combination of these models.

TABLE 4-1 Forest design models

Model	Description
Organizational	This model enables multiple forests to be created based on needs for user account and resource management. It can be used for service autonomy, and for service or data isolation.
Resource	This model uses a separate forest for management of resources only, with user accounts available only as needed for providing service accounts. It can be used for service isolation.
Restricted	This model uses a separate forest for user accounts and data that must be separate. It is frequently used for data isolation, and separate user accounts are needed.

> **MORE INFO** **MULTIPLE FORESTS**
>
> See *w* for additional considerations for multiple forests. Even though this document contains information on previous Windows versions, the concepts are still the same; this document was also cross-referenced from some of the Windows Server 2012 documentation.

Trusts

By default, users authenticate and can access resources in their domain. Trusts enable cross-domain and cross-forest resource access and authentication. Table 4-2 lists several trust relationships.

TABLE 4-2 Trust relationships

Trust Type	Transitive	Direction	Description
External	Non-transitive	One- or two-way	Provides access to resources in a Windows NT 4.0 domain or a domain in a separate forest
Forest	Transitive	One- or two-way	Provides access between forests
Realm	Transitive or non-transitive	One- or two-way	Provides a trust relationship to a non-Windows Kerberos realm
Shortcut	Transitive	One- or two-way	Provides improved logon times between domains in the same forest

An important concept to understand is *trust transitivity*, in which trust propagates between trusted resources to other resources. For example, when a forest trust is created between two forests in a transitive manner, that trust then extends to all domains within each forest.

Contrast this with a non-transitive trust, whereby the trust relationship exists solely between the domains participating in the relationship.

> **MORE INFO** **CREATING CERTAIN TRUST TYPES**
>
> See *http://technet.microsoft.com/en-us/library/cc771568* for more information on trusts, including discussing when to create certain trust types. For a description of shortcut trusts, see *http://technet.microsoft.com/library/cc754538*.

Functional levels

Functional levels refer to the features available to an Active Directory domain and forest as specifically compared to versions of Active Directory available with previous versions of Windows Server. For example, a forest functioning at the Windows Server 2008 level has added functionality, including greater control over password policies and additional logon information, when compared to a forest operating at the Windows Server 2003 level.

A minimum forest functional level of Windows Server 2003 is required to add Windows Server 2012 as a domain controller. Otherwise, the Windows Server 2012 forest functional level remains the same from Windows Server 2008 R2. At the domain functional level in Windows Server 2012, the support for Dynamic Access Control and Kerberos armoring KDC administrative template policy has two settings: Always Provide Claims and Full Unarmored Authentication Requests.

> **MORE INFO** **DOMAIN FUNCTIONAL LEVELS**
>
> See *http://technet.microsoft.com/library/cc771294.aspx* for more information on domain functional levels.

You can roll back the forest functional level from Windows Server 2012 to Windows Server 2008 R2. At the domain level, you generally can't roll back unless you've raised the domain functional level to Windows Server 2012 (or Windows Server 2008 R2) and still have the forest at the Windows Server 2008 level. In this case, you can roll the domain functional level back to Windows Server 2008 or Windows Server 2008 R2.

> **NOTE** **BACKUP AND RESTORE**
>
> As a last resort, you could use a backup and restore to get back to the previous functional level, although this isn't an official rollback in the true sense of the term.

Domain upgrade

Domain upgrade is the process of upgrading the domain from one version of Active Directory to another by upgrading the operating system. The operating system itself is upgraded, but the forest and domain functional levels still must be upgraded thereafter. The disk housing the Active Directory database (NTIS.DIT) is recommended to have at least 20 percent free disk space before beginning the operating system upgrade. Note that this process is distinct from a domain migration.

Performing a domain upgrade involves two primary methods: an in-place upgrade and a swing server upgrade. In the in-place upgrade, you upgrade the operating system on the actual running domain controllers. However, a more common scenario is the swing server upgrade, in which you add a Windows Server 2012 server to the domain as a domain controller and retire one of the legacy domain controllers. This process would continue until all domain controllers are replaced, after which time the forest functional level could be upgraded.

> **MORE INFO** **UPGRADING A DOMAIN**
>
> See *http://technet.microsoft.com/en-us/library/hh994618* for more information on upgrading a domain to Windows Server 2012.

Domain migration and forest restructure

Migrating domains means restructuring the resources between domains, either within or between forests. The Active Directory Migration Tool (ADMT) assists in domain migration. It can assist with interforest domain restructure, which migrates domains between forests, such as when two organizations merge. The ADMT tool can also assist with intraforest domain restructures, which are migrations of domains within a forest. This might be done to reduce overhead of managing multiple domains or to reflect organizational changes.

The considerations listed in Table 4-3 all pertain to domain migration.

TABLE 4-3 Domain migration considerations

Consideration	Interforest	Intraforest
Closed sets	Accounts in closed sets don't need to be migrated.	Accounts in closed sets must be migrated.
Local profile migration	ADMT must be used to migrate local profiles.	Local profiles are automatically migrated.
Object preservation	Objects are cloned; original remains in source location.	User and group objects are migrated and no longer exist at the source, whereas computer and service accounts are copied and exist both in the target and source.
Password retention	Optional	Retained
Security Identifier (SID) history	Optional	Required for user, group, and computer accounts but not service accounts.

Hybrid cloud services

A *hybrid cloud* is an infrastructure scenario that takes advantage of in-house resources as well as externally hosted resources located in the cloud. Access control and authentication are still necessary in the cloud, however; therefore, designing a cloud solution often requires duplicate resource management and deployments. With Windows Server 2012, you can extend Active Directory control into cloud-based platforms to provide hybrid cloud services through claims-based authorization.

When designing Active Directory services, you should pay attention to whether hybrid cloud services will be used and, if so, what resources and interaction will be necessary with Active Directory. You can virtualize Active Directory in Windows Server 2012 much more easily, thus enabling a domain controller to be deployed in a cloud-hosted environment.

THOUGHT EXPERIMENT
Enabling resource access

In the following thought experiment, apply what you've learned about this objective. You can find answers to these questions in the "Answers" section at the end of this chapter.

Your company has acquired another company that operates an Active Directory forest and domain for authentication. You've been tasked with coming up with a strategy for enabling users in both organizations to access resources in each other's domains. The deadline for the implementation is less than two weeks.

1. What type of strategy will you choose to enable this access?

2. If you choose a trust, what type of trust will you choose? If you choose a migration, what type of migration will you choose?

Objective summary

- Scenarios for operating a multi-forest architecture include doing so for autonomy of service management or data or for isolation of service management or data.
- Trust relationships enable resources in multiple forests and domains to be shared in a one- or two-way manner.

- Trusts passed on to child domains within a forest are called *transitive trusts*.
- *Hybrid cloud* refers to the ability of Windows Server 2012 to provide directory services to externally hosted cloud resources.
- You use domain upgrades to upgrade from earlier versions of Windows.
- Domain migrations and forest restructures refer to tasks related to moving resources between domains and forests.

Objective review

Answer the following questions to test your knowledge of the information in this objective. You can find the answers to these questions and explanations of why each answer choice is correct or incorrect in the "Answers" section at the end of this chapter.

1. What type of trust should be created for improving user logon times?

    A. Domain

    B. Forest

    C. External

    D. Shortcut

2. What type of multi-forest scenario is necessary for an organization that has stringent legal requirements for keeping management and access to resources separate?

    A. Service Autonomy

    B. Data Isolation

    C. Data and Service Isolation

    D. Data and Service Autonomy

3. What type of domain migration automatically retains user passwords?

    A. Interforest

    B. Intraforest

    C. Intradomain

    D. External

4. When strategies are compared for dividing up control within an Active Directory structure, what type of strategy is less expensive?

    A. Isolation

    B. Autonomy

    C. Interforest

    D. Intraforest

Objective 4.2: Implement a forest and domain infrastructure

As one of the broadest objective areas on the 70-413 exam, implementing a forest and domain infrastructure is arguably one of the areas that professional-level engineers and architects are most familiar with.

This objective covers:

- Configure domain rename
- Configure Kerberos realm trusts
- Implement a domain upgrade
- Implement a domain migration
- Implement a forest restructure
- Deploy and manage a test forest, including synchronization with production forests

Configuring domain rename

Renaming a domain involves several preliminary steps, in addition to the steps involved in actually renaming the domain.

Preliminary steps for domain rename

Table 4-4 describes the preliminary steps involved in renaming a domain.

TABLE 4-4 Preparation steps for renaming a domain

Step	Description
1. Adjust forest functional level	To rename a domain, on the domain controller you must first verify the forest functional level or raise it, if necessary. This task is accomplished in the Active Directory Domains and Trusts console. Within Active Directory Domains and Trusts, right-click Active Directory Domains and Trusts in the scope pane and select Raise Forest Functional Level from the context menu.
	If the current forest functional level is already at Windows Server 2012, this task is complete. Otherwise, select an available level and click Raise. See *http://technet.microsoft.com/library/cc794904* for more information.
2. Create any short-cut trust relationships	This step is necessary if you are restructuring domains within the forest. See *http://technet.microsoft.com/library/cc794918* for more information.
3. Prepare DNS zones	Make changes to the relevant DNS zones for the rename. See *http://technet.microsoft.com/en-us/library/cc794811* for more information.
4. Relocate folder redirection and roaming user profiles	This step is necessary only if you're using folder redirection or roaming profiles. See *http://technet.microsoft.com/en-us/library/cc794753* for more information.

Step	Description
5. Prepare member computers for host-name change	The DNS suffix changes as part of a domain rename, and some computers may need to be configured to handle the name change. See *http://technet.microsoft .com/en-us/library/cc816608* for more information.
6. Prepare Certification Authorities	You can prepare the certificate authorities (CAs) within the organization to continue through the rename process. See *http://technet.microsoft.com/en-us/library/ cc816587* for more information.
7. Prepare Exchange	Microsoft Exchange involves several limitations and special requirements. The extra steps are described at *http://technet.microsoft.com/en-us/library/cc794909.*

Steps for domain rename

Performing the actual rename of the domain involves several steps. Three command-line tools are also required for the rename:

- Rendom.exe
- Repadmin.exe
- Gpfixup.exe

These tools are part of the Remote Server Administration Tools feature, which you can install as a feature in Windows Server 2012 or download for Windows 8. Table 4-5 describes the steps involved to rename a domain.

NOTE **RUNNING THESE COMMANDS**

You need to run the commands in this section from a staging computer, using an account that has Domain Admin privileges.

TABLE 4-5 Renaming a domain

Step	Description
1. Perform a backup of all domain controllers	You should perform a full system state backup of all domain controllers before beginning the rename.
2. Configure an administrative computer	An administrative computer will maintain control over the rename. This computer should be a member of the domain but not a domain controller. This computer needs copies of the aforementioned command-line tools, which you can install with the Remote Server Administration Tools feature in Windows Server 2012. See *http://technet.microsoft.com/library/cc816869* for more information and *http://www.microsoft.com/download/details.aspx?id=28972* to download the tools for Windows 8.
3. Freeze the forest configuration	You need to stop activities such as adding domain controllers, adding domains, or making other domain- or forest-level changes before beginning the process. See *http://technet.microsoft.com/library/cc816725* for more information.

Step	Description
4. Generate forest description	This step begins the heart of the rename operation. Here, you generate a file called Domanlist.xml that contains a description of the forest. You do so in the current forest by using the command random.exe /list. See *http://technet .microsoft.com/library/cc794807* for more information.
5. Create new forest description	In this step, you edit the Domainlist.xml file created in the preceding step to specify details about the new forest. See *http://technet.microsoft.com/library/ cc816795* for additional details on this step.
6. Generate domain rename instructions	This step uses random.exe to create the domain rename instructions. The ren-dom /upload command creates a file called Dclist.xml in the current directory.
7. Push domain rename instructions	In this step, you replicate the domain rename instructions to all domain con-trollers using the repadmin command: `repadmin /syncall /d /e /P /q <domain master>` where <domain master> is the primary server responsible for the domain.
8. Verify domain controller readiness.	This step uses the rendom.exe tool to verify that the domain control-lers are ready to execute the domain rename process. The command is random /prepare, and the process updates the file Dclist.xml. In that file, each domain controller should be in the Prepared state.
9. Run domain rename	With the domain controllers prepared, running the command random /execute begins the rename process. When the command completes, you can look through the Dclist.xml file for the Done state or an Error state for the domain controllers involved in the renaming process.
10. Update Exchange	If necessary, run the XDR-fixup tool for Exchange. See *http://technet.microsoft .com/library/cc794842* for more information.
11. Unfreeze the forest configuration	Run random /end to thaw the forest.

After the process completes, if you have any external trusts, you'll need to reestablish them. Specifically, interforest trusts and external trusts with a domain in another forest will need to be redone. Also, you might need to fix Group Policy Objects (GPOs) by using the Gpfixup.exe tool.

> ***MORE INFO*** **GPFIXUP.EXE SYNTAX**
>
> See *http://technet.microsoft.com/library/cc816765* for more information and specific syntax for this command.

After running rendom /upload, the Dclist.xml file contains content similar to the following. Notice particularly the <state> set to Initial in this example:

```xml
<?xml version ="1.0"?>
<DcList>
    <Hash>n2etuL1E+eIxFRBC1noUlOuEidc=</Hash>
    <Signature>8azMQMMe7G/iKOFBLYVeneNv/Pk=</Signature>
    <DC>
        <Name>WINSRV13.adventure-works.com</Name>
        <State>Initial</State>
        <Password></Password>
        <LastError>0</LastError>
        <LastErrorMsg></LastErrorMsg>
        <FatalErrorMsg></FatalErrorMsg>
        <Retry></Retry>
    </DC>
</DcList>
```

Then after running repadmin and then rendom /prepare, the Dclist.xml file looks like this (again, notice the <state> field, which is now set to Prepared):

```xml
<?xml version ="1.0"?>
<DcList>
    <Hash>aK+MCmYdleL8fivp7xV63eyByt8=</Hash>
    <Signature>HJuoZ/GFECUm3lLfipI8gKZrtw8=</Signature>
    <DC>
        <Name>WINSRV13.adventure-works.com</Name>
        <State>Prepared</State>
        <Password>CKzpiTabHUk=</Password>
        <LastError>0</LastError>
        <LastErrorMsg></LastErrorMsg>
        <FatalErrorMsg></FatalErrorMsg>
        <Retry></Retry>
    </DC>
</DcList>
```

Finally, after running rendom /execute, the <state> changes to Done:

```xml
<?xml version ="1.0"?>
<DcList>
    <Hash>aK+MCmYdleL8fivp7xV63eyByt8=</Hash>
    <Signature>HJuoZ/GFECUm3lLfipI8gKZrtw8=</Signature>
    <DC>
    <Name>WINSRV13.adventure-works.com</Name>
        <State>Done</State>
        <Password>CKzpiTabHUk=</Password>
        <LastError>0</LastError>
        <LastErrorMsg></LastErrorMsg>
        <FatalErrorMsg></FatalErrorMsg>
        <Retry></Retry>
    </DC>
</DcList>
```

Configuring a Kerberos realm trust

Realm trusts enable connectivity between Windows Server 2012 running Active Directory and other systems, such as UNIX and Linux running a Kerberos-compatible server. You establish a realm trust inside the Active Directory Domains and Trusts console.

Within the Active Directory Domains and Trusts console, right-clicking the domain for which the trust will be created and selecting Properties reveals that domain's Properties sheet. Within that Properties sheet, the Trusts tab contains information about trusts for the domain. See Figure 4-1 for an example of this tab.

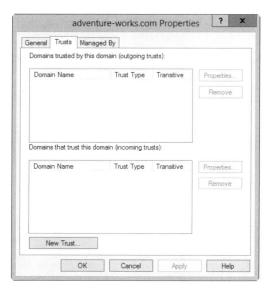

FIGURE 4-1 Use the Trusts tab to work with and create new trusts.

Clicking New Trust begins the New Trust Wizard. The first step of the New Trust Wizard involves entering the domain to be trusted in the Name text box, as shown in Figure 4-2.

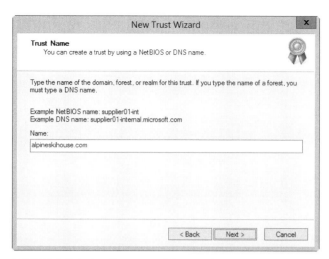

FIGURE 4-2 Entering the name of the new trust.

Next, you select the trust type, which should be set to Realm Trust, as shown in Figure 4-3.

FIGURE 4-3 Setting the trust type.

You set the trust's transitivity next, as shown in Figure 4-4. You can set the transitivity according to the organizational needs for this trust.

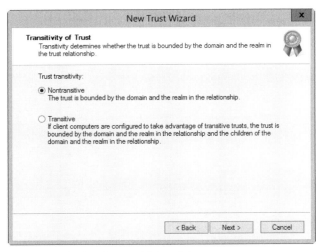

FIGURE 4-4 Setting the transitivity of the trust.

The direction for the trust is set next (see Figure 4-5), again to be set according to the organization's needs.

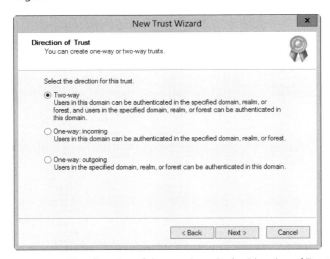

FIGURE 4-5 The direction of the trust is set in the Direction of Trust dialog box.

Next, the trust password is set, as shown in Figure 4-6.

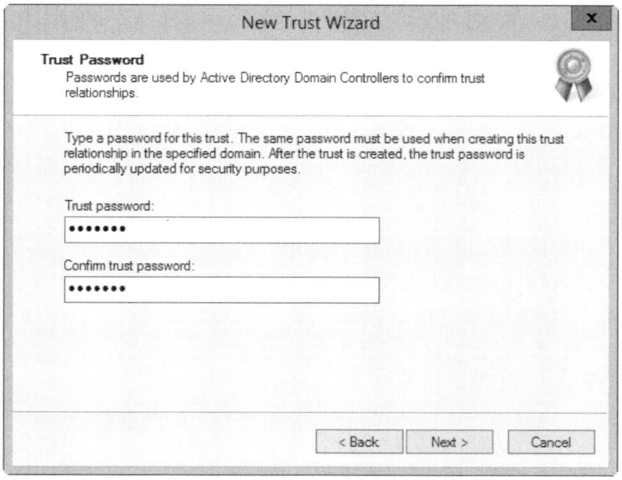

FIGURE 4-6 Setting the password for the trust.

With that configuration, the trust is created within the Windows domain. Configuration also needs to occur on the Kerberos server responsible for the domain being trusted. This configuration depends on the Kerberos implementation.

Once the trust is created, you can change it at any time on the Trusts tab of the domain's Properties sheet. You also can configure support for Kerberos AES encryption within the trust's properties, as shown in Figure 4-7.

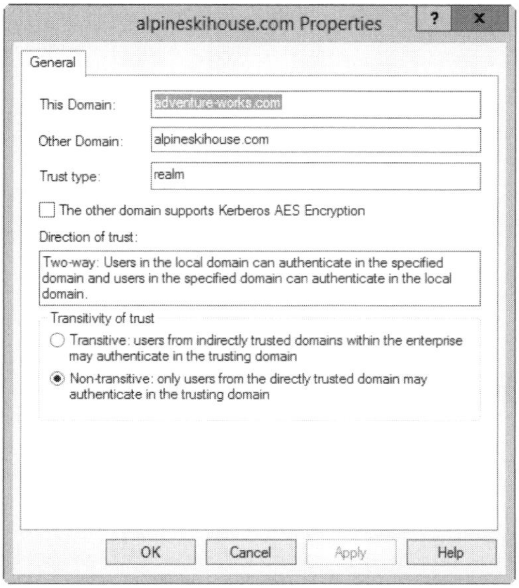

FIGURE 4-7 Properties for a trust.

Implementing a domain upgrade

Domain upgrades update the operational level of a domain, such as would happen when upgrading from Windows Server 2008 R2 to Windows Server 2012. Windows Server 2003 forest functional level is the minimum forest functional level eligible for upgrade to Windows Server 2012.

In previous versions of Windows, upgrading a domain meant running the adprep command with several options to prepare the server for the upgrade.

A domain upgrade occurs during the role installation process, during which you first choose to add the new Windows Server 2012 to an existing domain (see Figure 4-8).

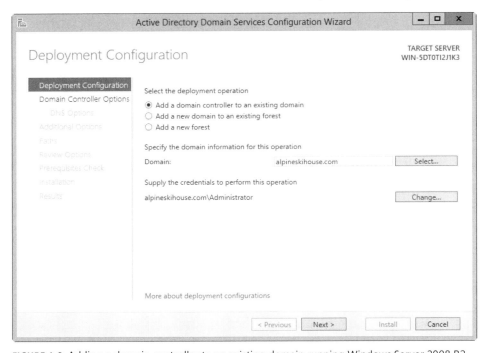

FIGURE 4-8 Adding a domain controller to an existing domain running Windows Server 2008 R2.

The next several panes in the wizard are the same as the default Configuration Wizard process, specifying the domain controller options and paths for the database, log files, and SYSVOL. Of note is the suboption underneath Paths, called Preparation Options. This pane, shown in Figure 4-9, indicates that the wizard will run forest and domain preparation commands as part of the installation.

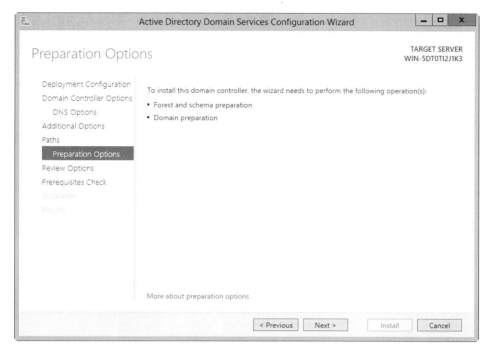

FIGURE 4-9 The Configuration Wizard needs to prepare the forest and schema when upgrading a domain.

Once complete, the wizard installs the AD DS Domain Controller and reboots the server.

Implementing a domain migration

The Active Directory Migration Tool (ADMT) is central to implementing a domain migration. ADMT requires a SQL Server installation, which can be SQL Server Express or an existing SQL Server in the organization.

The ADMT tool has several wizards to assist in migration, depending on the type of object to be migrated. As discussed earlier, domain migrations come in two forms: interforest for objects moving between domains in two separate forests, and intraforest for objects moving between domains within a forest.

Table 4-6 describes the general steps for implementing an interforest migration.

TABLE 4-6 Steps for implementing an interforest migration

Step	Description
1. Enable firewall exception	Enable the File and Printer Sharing exception in Windows Firewall between the domain controllers responsible for the forest.
2. Prepare source and target domains	This step, with several substeps, involves establishing trusts and migration accounts as well as configuring Security Identifier (SID) history, the target domain's Organizational Unit (OU) structure, and installing ADMT in the target domain. See *http://technet.microsoft.com/en-us/library/cc974324* and *http://technet.microsoft.com/en-us/library/cc974370* for more information.
3. Specify and transition service accounts	This step uses the Service Account Migration Wizard in ADMT. See *http://technet.microsoft.com/library/cc974375* for more information.
4. Migrate global groups	Use the Group Account Migration Wizard. See *http://technet.microsoft.com/library/cc974366* for more information.
5. Migrate other accounts	Migrate managed service, user, and workstation accounts with their SID histories. See *http://technet.microsoft.com/library/cc974384*, *http://technet.microsoft.com/library/migrating-managed-service-accounts*, and *http://technet.microsoft.com/library/cc974368* for information on this step.
6. Migrate resources	This step migrates member servers and domain local groups. See *http://technet.microsoft.com/library/cc974395* for more information.
7. Add SIDs to Access Control Lists (ACLs) in the target	This step translates the security on servers to add the user and groups accounts to the ACLs. See *http://technet.microsoft.com/library/cc974439* for more information.
8. Perform a remigration	User accounts, workstation computers, and member servers need to be remigrated at this step. See *http://technet.microsoft.com/library/cc974395* for more information.
9. Migrate domain local groups	Work with domain local groups as part of the migration process. See *http://technet.microsoft.com/en-us/library/cc974343* for more information.
10. Migrate domain controllers	Work with domain controllers as part of the migration process. See *http://technet.microsoft.com/library/cc974428* for more information.
11. Translate security and decommission source	In this post-migration step, you translate security on member servers and decommission the source domain. See *http://technet.microsoft.com/library/cc974389* and *http://technet.microsoft.com/library/cc974338* for more information.

Implementing a forest restructure

Forest restructuring involves moving a domain within a forest. Any domain within a forest can be moved, with the exception of the forest root domain. You use the rendom tool to restructure a forest. First, you generate a Domainlist.xml file with rendom /list, edit the file, run rendom /upload to send it to the servers, run rendom /prepare to prepare the servers, and finally use rendom /execute to implement the change.

A domain migration is sometimes also considered a forest restructure, specifically an intraforest migration. Table 4-7 describes how to perform an intraforest migration.

TABLE 4-7 Steps for performing an intraforest migration

Step	Description
1. Enable firewall exception	Enable the File and Printer Sharing exception in Windows Firewall between the domain controllers responsible for the forest.
2. Prepare source and target domains	This step, with several substeps, involves assigning domain object roles and locations, installing ADMT in the target, creating migration account groups, and performing other tasks. See *http://technet.microsoft.com/library/cc974347* and *http://technet.microsoft.com/library/cc974370* for more information.
3. Migrate universal and global groups	This step involves the Group Account Migration Wizard. See *http://technet.microsoft.com/library/cc974386* for more information.
4. Migrate service accounts	This step uses the Service Account Migration Wizard in ADMT. See *http://technet.microsoft.com/library/cc974383* for more information.
5. Migrate managed service accounts	Work with managed service accounts as part of the migration process. See *http://technet.microsoft.com/library/migrating-managed-service-accounts* for more information.
6. Migrate user accounts	Work with user accounts as part of the migration process. See *http://technet.microsoft.com/library/cc974404* for more information.
7. Translate local user profiles	Translate local user profiles as part of the migration process. See *http://technet.microsoft.com/library/cc974340* for more information.
8. Migrate resources	Migrate workstation computers and member servers. See *http://technet.microsoft.com/library/cc974402* for more information.
9. Migrate domain local groups	Migrate domain local groups as part of the process. See *http://technet.microsoft.com/library/cc974350* for more information.
10. Translate security and decommission source	In this post-migration step, you translate security on member servers and decommission the source domain. See *http://technet.microsoft.com/library/cc974405* and *http://technet.microsoft.com/library/cc974458* for more information.

> **MORE INFO**   **INTRAFOREST DOMAIN RESTRUCTURING**
>
> See *http://technet.microsoft.com/library/cc974371* for more information on an intraforest domain restructure.

Deploying and managing a test forest

A test forest is considered a best practice. You can use a test forest to implement changes to an Active Directory schema safely by isolating those changes from the production forest or to implement software upgrades in an isolated environment. Using a test forest for software upgrades enables dependent software, such as Lync or SharePoint, to be tested with the new software before rolling it out to the production environment.

Deploying a test forest means adding the Active Directory Domain Services (AD DS) role and then running the AD DS Configuration Wizard to create a new forest. With the new forest created, you can synchronize things like Group Policy by using Group Policy Management.

You use the Migration Table Editor, shown in Figure 4-10, to migrate objects between domains in different forests (and between domains in the same forest).

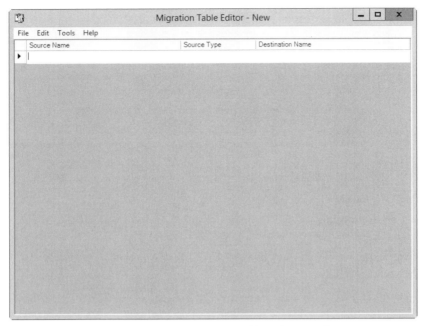

FIGURE 4-10 The Migration Table Editor migrates objects between forests.

MORE INFO **USING THE MIGRATION TABLE EDITOR**

For more information on using the Migration Table editor, see *http://technet.microsoft .com/library/cc754682*.

Follow these steps to migrate settings between a test and production forest:

1. Install the new forest domain controller using the Active Directory Domain Services Configuration Wizard.

2. Establish a trust between the two forests by using Active Directory Domains and Trusts.

3. In Group Policy Management, add the test forest by selecting Add Forest from the Group Policy Management Actions list.

4. Copy objects as necessary for synchronization.

MORE INFO **MANAGING GROUP POLICY OBJECTS**

See *http://technet.microsoft.com/en-us/library/cc754760* for more information on manag-ing Group Policy Objects.

THOUGHT EXPERIMENT
Adding a new domain

In the following thought experiment, apply what you've learned about this objective. You can find answers to these questions in the "Answers" section at the end of this chapter.

Your organization will be partnering with another firm. As part of the partnership, you need to restructure the forest to add the partner's domain.

Describe the steps involved in this restructuring process.

Objective summary

- Kerberos realm trusts are established through Active Directory Domains and Trusts via the New Trust Wizard.
- You can use test forests to implement changes in the Active Directory schema in such a way that they don't interfere with the production Active Directory implementation.
- Domain upgrades with Windows Server 2012 are completed using a wizard when the Active Directory Domain Services role is installed.
- Test forests are typically used to provide a safe place to make changes to things like Group Policy without having to change the production forest.

Objective review

Answer the following questions to test your knowledge of the information in this objective. You can find the answers to these questions and explanations of why each answer choice is correct or incorrect in the "Answers" section at the end of this chapter.

1. You're establishing a realm trust and the domain to which you're connecting supports Kerberos AES Encryption. Where is this configured on the Windows Server 2012 domain?

   A. In the New Trust Wizard, on the Password and Encryption dialog box

   B. In the New Trust Wizard, on the Trust Domain dialog box

   C. In the trust's Properties sheet

   D. In the Computer Domain Trust Properties sheet

2. Renaming a forest involves several commands. Identify the command you use to create the Domainlist.xml file.

   A. repadmin /list

   B. domainlist /generate

   C. rendom /list

   D. dcdiag /create

3. Restructuring a forest uses which of the following commands?

   A. Rendom.exe

   B. Adprep.exe

   C. Adrestructure.exe

   D. Forestadmin.exe

Objective 4.3: Design a Group Policy strategy

Group Policy applies security and other computer configuration settings based on granular criteria within an organization. Because the level of control is quite granular and the rules to be applied can be very complex, the design of Group Policy is very important. For example, having too many GPOs can slow down logons significantly.

This objective looks at design of Group Policy in an enterprise, focusing on the areas specified in the 70-413 exam objectives. Central to design of Group Policy is designing an Organizational Unit (OU) structure that supports the organization's Group Policy needs. The infrastructure such as Active Directory and other lower-level prerequisites also must all be in place for Group Policy design to take place.

This objective covers:

- Design considerations, including inheritance blocking, enforced policies, loopback processing, security and Windows Management Instrumentation (WMI) filtering, site-linked Group Policy Objects (GPOs), slow-link processing, group strategies, Organization Unit (OU) hierarchy, and Advanced Group Policy Management (AGPM)

Blocking inheritance

Group Policy Objects (GPOs) linked to higher levels in a structure are, by default, passed down or inherited to lower levels in the model. This can be overridden at a lower level in the structure. For example, you might apply a desktop security policy for the organization as a whole but apply a more stringent policy to a specific domain in the organization. You can achieve this by linking a GPO to the lower-level domain.

To prevent the default inheritance behavior, implement a Block Inheritance policy, which prevents higher-level linked GPOs from being applied. You should use this sparingly, however, because it can make troubleshooting difficult, so although this option is available and you should be aware that it is possible, use this option only as necessary when designing your Group Policy.

Using enforced policies

Closely related to inheritance blocking are enforced policies. You can't override an enforced policy at lower levels. In the case of the preceding desktop security policy example, if you set a policy at the top level of the OU, it can't be overridden at a lower level when the link is designated as Enforced.

Like with inheritance blocking, it's recommended that you use enforced policies sparingly.

Using loopback processing

Loopback processing is used in special cases in which the computer must have the same policy and environment regardless of who logs on. Think of a loopback process as a way to apply group policy to a computer rather than an individual user. You could use this setting in a public kiosk setting or a reception area.

Loopback processing is configured within the Group Policy Management Console (GPMC) in the User Group Policy loopback process mode policy setting (in the Computer Configuration\Policies\Administrative Templates\System\Group Policy hierarchy). This setting has two modes of operation:

- **Merge mode**   The user's and computer's GPOs are merged, and any conflicting poli-cies use the computer's policy to override the user's setting.
- **Replace mode**   The user's GPOs aren't gathered at all; only the computer's GPOs are applied.

Using Windows Management Instrumentation (WMI) filters

You can also use Windows Management Instrumentation (WMI) filters to determine the scope of a GPO application. WMI filters do this based on the computer's attributes to which the policy is being applied. When WMI filters are processed, the GPO is applied only if the filter evaluates to true.

WMI filters allow for granular access to apply GPOs to the specific computer or user level based on information from the target computer. For example, WMI can determine which services are running and apply only to computers with a specific service running, or WMI can be used to apply GPOs to certain types of computers. WMI can also examine the hardware configuration, registry, and other settings and can be applied based on its findings related to those settings.

The drawback to WMI filters is that they are evaluated each time Group Policy is pro-cessed, thus adding overhead to the logon time. Only one WMI filter is allowed per GPO.

Understanding site-linked GPOs

GPOs linked at the site level can be used for printers, proxy and network settings, or other settings related to a specific site. The GPOs linked at a site container level apply to all comput-ers at that site regardless of domain or forest membership. The following recommendations are related to site-linked GPOs:

- To manage site GPOs, you need to be a member of the Enterprise Admins or Domain Admins group in the forest root.
- Replication for domain controllers in different sites occurs less frequently than replica-tion within a site.
- Replication for domain controllers in different sites occurs only during scheduled replication periods, which by default is set to three hours and is set in the Inter-Site Transports section of Active Directory Sites and Services.
- Care should be taken to ensure that GPOs aren't accessed across a wide area network (WAN) link for performance reasons, although this can be mitigated with slow link processing, as discussed in the next section.

Using slow link processing

Group Policy should not be applied when the connection speed between the domain controller and the computer obtaining the policy falls below a certain threshold. You can configure the settings for slow links, so if your design will include computers obtaining Group Policy across a slow network link, you should plan accordingly. The default slow link rate is 500 kbps (kilobits per second).

The link speed is detected by using Network Location Awareness (NLA) during the preprocessing phase of Group Policy processing. When a slow link is detected, not all group policy components are processed. Table 4-8 lists components and whether each is processed when a slow link has been detected.

TABLE 4-8 Which components process when a slow link is detected

Setting	Processed
802.3 Group Policy	Yes
Administrative Templates	Yes (can't be disabled)
Deployed Printer Connections	No
Disk Quotas	No
EFS	Yes
Folder Redirection	No
Group Policy Preferences	Yes
IE maintenance	Yes
Internet Explorer Zone Mapping	Yes
IP Security	Yes
Microsoft Offline Files	Yes
QoS Packet Scheduler	Yes
Scripts	No
Security	Yes (can't be disabled)
Software Installation	No
Software Restriction Policies	Yes
Windows Search	Yes
Wireless	Yes

You can configure the slow link speed for computers or users in Policies\Administrative Templates\System\Group Policy in either the Computer Configuration or User Configuration container, respectively. The setting, called Group Policy Slow Link Detection, is measured in

Kbps. The setting can also be applied for User Profiles within the Computer Configuration\Policies\Administrative Templates\System\User Profiles container and is called Slow Network Connection Timeout For User Profiles.

The Do Not Detect Slow Network Connections policy setting disables slow link detection.

Processed as client-side extensions, the computer policy can be large, which can negatively affect performance on a slow link. By default, only the Administrative templates and security-related policy settings are processed when a slow link has been detected. The Allow Processing Across A Slow Network Connection setting is used to control processing of these extensions on a slow link.

Understanding group strategies

You can use security filtering to apply GPOs to selected groups in Active Directory. For example, you might want to prevent certain GPOs from applying to certain groups, like the Administrators group. In this case, you'd use the Scope tab within Security Filtering in the GPO's details pane to remove "Authenticated Users" and then add the specific groups to which the GPO should be applied.

Understanding OU hierarchy

GPOs are usually linked at the OU level, so ensuring that the OU hierarchy supports a GPO structure is key. The OU hierarchy should reflect the administrative structure of the organization, and a properly designed OU hierarchy can make delegation of administrative rights possible. When designing the OU hierarchy, you should make the objects to be managed a primary concern. For example, the structure may be based on geography, with an OU for each location, and child OUs are created only when it makes sense for application of Group Policy or for delegation.

Using Advanced Group Policy Management

Advanced Group Policy Management (AGPM) is part of the Microsoft Desktop Optimization Pack (MDOP). As the name implies, AGPM enables much more advanced control over Group Policy than the standard Group Policy Management Console. For example, AGPM enables you to edit GPOs in a staging environment and then deploy the changes to production, with rollback capabilities. AGPM enables change control so that tracking and auditing can occur.

> **NOTE** **MODP LICENSING**
>
> MDOP is licensed as part of Software Assurance.

AGPM can use role-based delegation so that one person can edit the GPOs while another person approves and deploys. Specifically, AGPM has three roles: Reviewer, Editor, and

Approver. The Reviewer role can view GPOs, while the Editor role can make changes. The Approver role can deploy the GPO to the production environment.

When you're designing a Group Policy strategy, consider whether these features are required in your organization and, if they are, plan on including AGPM in your design.

> **MORE INFO** **AGPM**
>
> See *http://www.microsoft.com/en-us/windows/enterprise/products-and-technologies/mdop/ agpm.aspx* for more information on AGPM.

THOUGHT EXPERIMENT
Group Policy strategy

I n the following thought experiment, apply what you've learned about this objective. You can find answers to these questions in the "Answers" section at the end of this chapter.

You're in charge of designing Group Policy for your organization, which consists of a single forest with three domains spread over two sites. The sites are connected via DS3 WAN links. One site contains both administrative personnel and research personnel. The research personnel are in their own domain that, due to the nature of their work, needs stronger security than the other domains.

Describe the Group Policy design strategy that you'll use for this topology, including how you'll apply more stringent policies to the high-security domain.

Objective summary

- Inheritance blocking prevents higher-level policies from being inherited at a lower level.
- Enforced policies prevent policies from being overridden at lower levels.
- You use loopback processing to create the same environment on a computer, regardless of who logs on to the computer.
- You can use Advanced Group Policy Management (AGPM) in a design where a formal review process is required.
- AGPM is part of the Microsoft Desktop Optimization Pack (MDOP).
- The Organizational Unit (OU) hierarchy is a key element to spend time on when creating a design.
- Group Policy measures link speed and, when the speed is measured under 500 kbps, slow-link processing takes effect.

Objective review

Answer the following questions to test your knowledge of the information in this objective. You can find the answers to these questions and explanations of why each answer choice is correct or incorrect in the "Answers" section at the end of this chapter.

1. Which of the following isn't processed when the slow-link rules are in effect?

   A. Administrative Templates

   B. Security

   C. Microsoft Offline Files

   D. Software Installation

2. Scheduled replication is by default set at which value for the Inter-Site Transport?

   A. 5 minutes

   B. 8 hours

   C. 1 day

   D. 3 hours

3. Of the processed policy components, which of the following can't be disabled when customizing the rules?

   A. IP Security

   B. Security

   C. Administrative Templates

   D. Windows Search

Objective 4.4: Design an Active Directory permission model

You can use a properly designed Active Directory permission model to spread the administrative overhead of management among multiple roles and locations.

This objective covers:
- Understanding design considerations, including Active Directory object security and Active Directory quotas
- Customizing tasks to delegate in Delegation of Control Wizard
- Deploying administrative tools on the client computer
- Delegating permissions on administrative users (AdminSDHolder)
- Configuring Kerberos delegation

Understanding design considerations for Active Directory permissions

Access Control Lists (ACLs) protect Active Directory objects. In much the same way that objects such as files have security applied to them, so too can objects in Active Directory. An object's security can be viewed in Active Directory Users and Computers on the Security tab of the Properties sheet. If the Properties sheet doesn't have a Security tab, select Advanced Features from the View menu in Active Directory Users and Computers to enable it. Figure 4-11 shows the Security tab for a computer object.

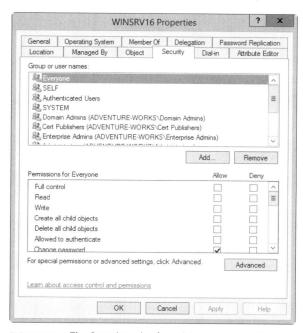

FIGURE 4-11 The Security tab of an object in Active Directory.

You can manage security for Active Directory objects at the object level or at the property level.

> **MORE INFO   OBJECT SECURITY**
>
> See *http://technet.microsoft.com/library/Cc977989* and *http://technet.microsoft.com/library/cc961985.aspx* for more information on object security.

Active Directory quotas mitigate denial-of-service attacks by limiting the number of objects that a security principal can own or create. You can apply quotas on the security principals at the partition level, such as on domain or application partitions.

Of note when applying quotas is that deleted objects (known as *tombstone objects*) count toward the quota, even though you can change the percentage of which are applied to the quota with the msDS-TombstoneQuotaFactor attribute found in the NTDS Quotas container. The value is set to 100 by default, meaning that 100 percent of tombstoned items count against the quota.

During the design of Active Directory permissions, one consideration surrounds high-security objects. For example, the design could prevent those with lower security rights, such as help desk staff, from changing high-security passwords.

MORE INFO   **QUOTAS**

See *http://technet.microsoft.com/library/cc904295* for more information on quotas.

Customizing tasks in the Delegation of Control Wizard

The Delegation of Control Wizard, found in Active Directory Users and Computers, shares the control of objects and roles among others in an organization. You can delegate control over objects to groups or individuals. For example, you might delegate the ability to reset user passwords to help-desk staff. You can also customize a complex delegation to meet your organization's needs.

In the Delegation of Control Wizard, after you choose the user or group, selecting Create A Custom Task To Delegate on the Tasks to Delegate dialog box begins the process of customizing the delegation. Figure 4-12 shows this dialog box.

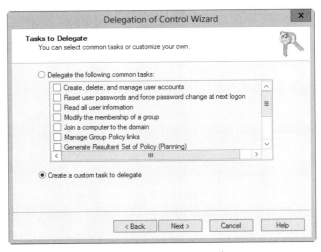

FIGURE 4-12 Choosing to create a custom task.

You next choose the objects to which this delegation will apply, as shown in Figure 4-13.

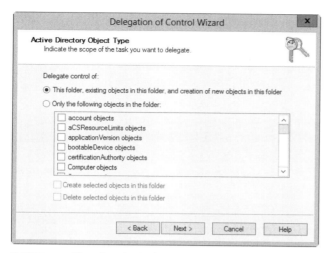

FIGURE 4-13 Choosing the Active Directory Object Type for this delegation.

Finally, you choose the permissions that will be used for this delegation. Figure 4-14 shows this dialog box.

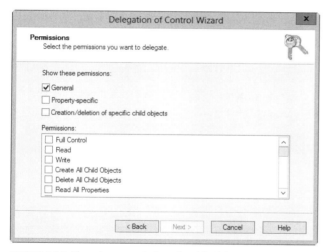

FIGURE 4-14 Choosing permissions for this delegation.

After you set up permissions, click Next to open a confirmation dialog box and create the delegation.

> **MORE INFO**   **DELEGATION OF CONTROL WIZARD**
>
> See *http://technet.microsoft.com/library/dd145344.aspx* for more information on the Delegation of Control Wizard.

Deploying Remote Server Administrative Tools on a client computer

You can install Remote Server Administration Tools (RSAT) as a Feature in Windows Server 2012. However, for Windows 8, RSAT is a separate download available at *http://www .microsoft.com/download/details.aspx?id=28972*.

Deployment of this package is accomplished on the client computer by double-clicking the installer, as detailed at *http://technet.microsoft.com/en-us/library/hh831501*.

Previous versions of RSAT required additional deployment to enable specific tools. The latest version of RSAT doesn't require this step; the tools are installed when the package itself is installed.

Delegating permissions on administrative users

The AdminSDHolder object rolls back to accounts that are part of a protected group, such as the Enterprise Admins group. The AdminSDHolder SDProp process watches for manual changes to protected accounts and overwrites them with a known-good permission set. However, sometimes you might like to enable a certain group—for example, to give a group of security administrators in the organization the ability to make changes to accounts protected by the AdminSDHolder object.

To delegate permissions, you need to change them on the AdminSDHolder object itself by using the ADSI Edit tool. Begin by opening ADSI Edit and connect to the Default naming context. Within the Default naming context, expand the DC to find CN=System.

Right-click CN=AdminSDHolder and select Properties. On the Properties sheet, click the Security tab to reveal the security for the object (see Figure 4-15).

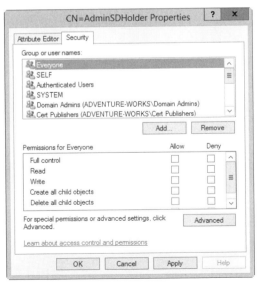

FIGURE 4-15 Security attributes on the CN=AdminSDHolder object.

Clicking Advanced reveals the Advanced Security Settings dialog box, as shown in Figure 4-16. Click Enable Inheritance in this dialog box and then click Apply.

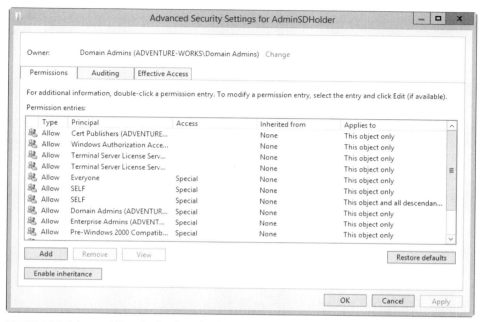

FIGURE 4-16 Advanced Security Settings for the CN=AdminSDHolder object.

Next, click Add. In the Permission Entry dialog box, select a principal that will obtain the permissions and then set the permissions themselves. For example, Figure 4-17 shows the Permission Entry dialog box with a group called the Rapid Response Team chosen as the principal. This group then is granted Full Control.

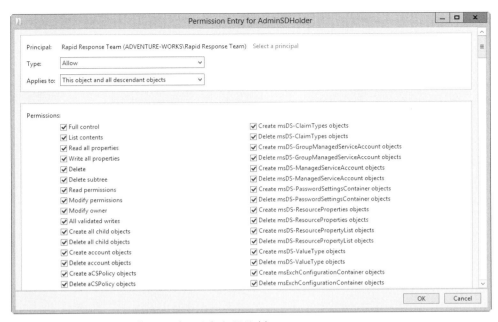

FIGURE 4-17 Delegating Full Control on AdminSDHolder to a group.

When the SDProp process executes again (by default every hour), these permissions are applied, and the Rapid Response Team gains Full Control over AdminSDHolder-managed objects.

Configuring Kerberos delegation

Kerberos delegation is configured in Active Directory Users and Computers by selecting the computer account that will be trusted for the delegation. Within that computer's Delegation tab of the Properties sheet, selecting either Trust This Computer For Delegation To Any Service (Kerberos Only) or Trust This Computer For Delegation To Specified Services Only and then selecting the Use Kerberos Only radio button results in Kerberos delegation being configured for the computer in question. This is shown in Figure 4-18.

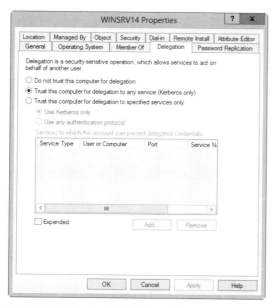

FIGURE 4-18 Configuring Kerberos delegation for a computer account.

You should also verify that the service account (and any other account used in the delegation) is enabled for delegation. This is accomplished within the user's Account tab of the Properties sheet (see Figure 4-19). Specifically, the Account Is Sensitive And Cannot Be Delegated box within the Account Options section can't be selected.

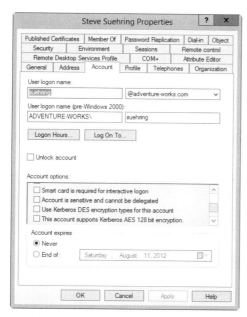

FIGURE 4-19 Ensuring that the Account Is Sensitive And Cannot Be Delegated box is cleared.

MORE INFO   **KERBEROS AND DELEGATION**

See *http://technet.microsoft.com/library/4a1daa3e-b45c-44ea-a0b6-fe8910f92f28* for more information on Kerberos, including delegation.

THOUGHT EXPERIMENT
Creating a new security group

In the following thought experiment, apply what you've learned about this objective. You can find answers to these questions in the "Answers" section at the end of this chapter.

You're creating a new department to manage security within your organization. This department will be responsible for emergency incident investigation and as such needs to be able to work with any accounts in Active Directory.

Describe the steps necessary to ensure that this group of users has access to accomplish their jobs.

Objective summary

- Active Directory object security refers to the security permissions that you can apply to all objects in Active Directory.
- You use Active Directory quotas to prevent a rogue security principal from creating extraneous objects, thereby potentially filling the disk on which the Active Directory database is housed.
- The Delegation of Control Wizard enables certain groups or individuals in an organization to share some responsibility for management of various aspects of an Active Directory implementation.
- Remote Server Administration Tools are available as a Feature in Windows Server 2012 and as an update package for Windows 8.
- You configure Kerberos delegation at the computer level and need to use additional configuration to ensure that each account object is allowed to be delegated.

Objective review

Answer the following questions to test your knowledge of the information in this objective. You can find the answers to these questions and explanations of why each answer choice is correct or incorrect in the "Answers" section at the end of this chapter.

1. At what level does Microsoft recommend placing quotas?

    A. At the forest level

    B. At the object level

    C. At the partition level

    D. At the permission level

2. The percentage of tombstone objects applied to a quota is configured with which attribute?

    A. msDS-TombstoneQuotaFactor

    B. msDS-TombstoneQuota

    C. msDS-QuotaTombstoneFactor

    D. msDS-TombstoneQuotaPercent

3. How often does the AdminSDHolder process SDProp run?

    A. 3 hours

    B. 1 day

    C. 1 hour

    D. 10 minutes

Chapter summary

- Several scenarios are available for working in a multi-forest architecture.
- Test forests provide a good way to try changes before rolling them into production.
- Group Policy design centers around enforcement of policies and their application within the domain.
- Advanced Group Policy Management (AGPM) is used where formal review processes are required.
- Designing Active Directory object security means working with security permissions for objects in Active Directory.

Answers

This section contains the solutions to the thought experiments and answers to the objective review questions in this chapter.

Objective 4.1: Thought experiment

1. Although you may end up restructuring the forests and merging them eventually, the timeline dictates that you use a trust.

2. You'll likely choose a two-way transitive forest trust because it enables each part of the organization to access resources in the other's forest and any domains within those forests.

Objective 4.1: Review

1. **Correct Answer:** D
   A. **Incorrect:** There's no Domain type trust.
   B. **Incorrect:** A forest trust doesn't affect logon times.
   C. **Incorrect:** An external trust establishes trust between domains but doesn't improve logon time.
   D. **Correct:** A shortcut trust helps improve logon times.

2. **Correct Answer:** C
   A. **Incorrect:** Service Autonomy doesn't provide isolation of resource access.
   B. **Incorrect:** Data Isolation provides isolation for resources but not for management of services.
   C. **Correct:** Data and Service Isolation isolates both resource access and management of services.
   D. **Incorrect:** Data and Service Autonomy doesn't provide separation.

3. **Correct Answer:** B
   A. **Incorrect:** An interforest migration can retain passwords but does not do so automatically.
   B. **Correct:** An intraforest migration automatically retains passwords.
   C. **Incorrect:** Intradomain isn't a migration scenario.
   D. **Incorrect:** External isn't a migration scenario.

4. **Correct Answer:** B

    A. **Incorrect:** Isolation requires duplication of resources and administration and is thus more expensive.

    B. **Correct:** Autonomy uses resources more efficiently to lessen administrative overhead.

    C. **Incorrect:** Interforest isn't a strategy for dividing control.

    D. **Incorrect:** Intraforest isn't a strategy for dividing control.

Objective 4.2: Thought experiment

Assuming that you have multiple child domains underneath a root-level forest, you would use the rendom /list command to create the Domainlist.xml file. You'd then make changes to that file to reflect the new structure and upload the file to the forest again to make the changes take effect.

Objective 4.2: Review

1. **Correct Answer:** C

    A. **Incorrect:** There's no Password and Encryption dialog box.

    B. **Incorrect:** You can't set encryption on the Trust Domain dialog box.

    C. **Correct:** AES Encryption is set within the trust's Properties sheet after initial configuration.

    D. **Incorrect:** There's no Computer Domain Trust Properties sheet.

2. **Correct Answer:** C

    A. **Incorrect:** repadmin /list isn't used to create the Domainlist.xml file.

    B. **Incorrect:** domainlist /generate isn't a real command.

    C. **Correct:** rendom /list creates the Domainlist.xml file.

    D. **Incorrect:** dcdiag /create isn't used to create a Domainlist.xml file.

3. **Correct Answer:** A

    A. **Correct:** Rendom.exe generates the list of domains and then uploads that list.

    B. **Incorrect:** Adprep.exe isn't used for this purpose.

    C. **Incorrect:** Adrestructure.exe isn't a real command.

    D. **Incorrect:** Forestadmin.exe isn't a real command.

Objective 4.3: Thought experiment

Design a hierarchical OU model that will use a standard set of Group Policy policies at the highest level and then likely inheritance blocking to apply more stringent rules as necessary in the high-security domain. Also, WMI filters might also need to be in place for that site, even for administrative computers, to apply any additional policies based on the location. Because the WAN links are DS3-based, the available bandwidth shouldn't be a problem, but the case setup didn't state anything about how saturated that WAN link already was, so it's likely that you would want to make sure that a domain controller is placed at that site if the WAN link is nearing capacity.

Objective 4.3: Review

1. **Correct Answer:** D
   A. **Incorrect:** Administrative templates are always processed.
   B. **Incorrect:** Security is always processed.
   C. **Incorrect:** Microsoft Offline Files are processed but can be disabled.
   D. **Correct:** Software Installation isn't processed by default but can be enabled.

2. **Correct Answer:** D
   A. **Incorrect:** 5 minutes isn't the correct value.
   B. **Incorrect:** 8 hours isn't the correct value.
   C. **Incorrect:** 1 day isn't the correct value.
   D. **Correct:** 3 hours is the default value for replication.

3. **Correct Answers:** B and C
   A. **Incorrect:** IP Security is enabled by default but can be disabled.
   B. **Correct:** Security can't be disabled.
   C. **Correct:** Administrative Templates can't be disabled.
   D. **Incorrect:** Windows Search can be disabled.

Objective 4.4: Thought experiment

Your first task is to create an Active Directory group that contains the members of this team. After that's complete, you need to change the AdminSDHolder object to ensure that the group has rights to make changes to privileged groups affected by the AdminSDHolder protection. This is accomplished in ADSI Edit.

Objective 4.4: Review

1. **Correct Answer:** C

   A. **Incorrect:** At the forest level isn't the correct place to apply quotas.

   B. **Incorrect:** At the object level isn't the correct place to apply quotas.

   C. **Correct:** At the partition level is the correct place to apply quotas.

   D. **Incorrect:** At the permission level isn't the correct place to apply quotas.

2. **Correct Answer:** A

   A. **Correct:** msDS-TombstoneQuotaFactor is the correct attribute for this percentage.

   B. **Incorrect:** msDS-TombstoneQuota isn't a real attribute.

   C. **Incorrect:** msDS-QuotaTombstoneFactor isn't a real attribute.

   D. **Incorrect:** msDS-TombstoneQuotaPercent isn't a real attribute.

3. **Correct Answer:** C

   A. **Incorrect:** 3 hours isn't the correct value.

   B. **Incorrect:** 1 day isn't the correct value.

   C. **Correct:** SDProp runs once an hour.

   D. **Incorrect:** 10 minutes isn't the correct value.

CHAPTER 5

Design and implement an Active Directory infrastructure (physical)

The final set of objectives in the 70-413 curriculum look at the physical design of an Active Directory infrastructure. Requirements for this area include things such as placement of Active Directory server roles and deployment of a branch office.

Objectives in this chapter:

- Objective 5.1: Design an Active Directory sites topology
- Objective 5.2: Design a domain controller strategy
- Objective 5.3: Design and implement a branch office infrastructure

Objective 5.1: Design an Active Directory sites topology

The site topology for Active Directory is the manifestation of the physical network topology. By designing a topology that reflects the network, including additional sites, while accounting for the usage at those sites, the Active Directory design can efficiently and reliably handle the resource needs of the organization.

This objective covers the following topics:

- Design considerations, including proximity of domain controllers, replication optimization, and site link
- Monitoring and resolving Active Directory replication conflicts

Understanding Active Directory topology design

Design of the Active Directory topology needs to consider the location of domain controllers, how data should be replicated between those domain controllers, and any additional links to sites.

When considering proximity of domain controllers, you need to examine four types of servers or roles:

- Forest root domain controller
- Regional domain controller
- Global catalog server
- Operations master role

The forest root domain controller, a term usually used in a multi-domain environment, enables access to resources between domains by creating trust paths between those domains. It's recommended that you place a forest root domain controller or create a shortcut trust in locations that have unreliable network connectivity.

Regional domain controllers provide local domain controller functionality at remote sites. You should place as few regional domain controllers on the network as possible. Regional domain controllers should be used at hub locations; Read-Only Domain Controllers (RODCs) are recommended in locations where physical security can't be guaranteed.

Global catalog servers and operations master roles are discussed further in Objective 5.2, "Design a domain controller strategy." In general, global catalog servers are required only when more than one forest is available.

> **MORE INFO**   **DOMAIN CONTROLLER PLACEMENT**
>
> See *http://technet.microsoft.com/library/cc754920* for more information on domain controller placement.

Active Directory uses multimaster, store-and-forward replication. Replication of data between sites is configured through a replication process built by the Active Directory Knowledge Consistency Checker (KCC). The KCC uses a least-cost spanning tree to optimize replication for bandwidth usage. Replication can be managed to further customize and configure its behavior, such as the schedule for replication.

Replication occurs differently depending on whether the traffic is passing within a site or between sites. Replication occurs on data updates within a site so that the change can become known within the site as quickly as possible. Replication between sites goes to a single domain controller in the remote site, which then further replicates the information to other domain controllers at that site.

Optimizing replication means analyzing the number of physical sites and comparing that against the available bandwidth between sites. Low speed (less than 10 Mbits) between sites calls for the establishment of multiple sites with domain controllers placed at those sites. You can configure various factors about replication such as the site link cost and frequency, which can further optimize replication based on the organization's needs and topology. You can adjust three primary factors to optimize replication configuration:

- Site cost
- Schedule
- Interval (180 minutes, by default)

> **MORE INFO**   **REPLICATION**
>
> See *http://technet.microsoft.com/library/cc731537* for more information on replication and *http://technet.microsoft.com/library/cc753700* for more information on managing properties related to replication.

It's recommended that you create sites for locations in which a domain controller is placed or in locations where the application requires a site to be created. An example of such an application is Distributed File System Namespaces (DFSN). Sites aren't necessarily tied to physical or geographical locations. Assuming that the available bandwidth and network latency is adequate (less than 10ms latency between locations is recommended), a single site can be used.

When sites are created, they are connected via a site link. Site links provide intersite connectivity for replication. Creating site links means creating a link in the Inter-Site Transports container and ensuring that every site is connected to each other. The same site link can be used for sites with the same connectivity and availability.

> **MORE INFO**   **SITE LINKS**
>
> See *http://technet.microsoft.com/library/cc732837* for more information on site links. Use the Geographic Locations and Communication Links worksheet available as part of the Windows Server 2003 Resource Kit and available at *http://www.microsoft.com/download/ details.aspx?id=9608* for assistance in topology design.

Monitoring and resolving Active Directory replication conflicts

Monitoring replication is accomplished through two command-line tools:

- repadmin /showrepl
- dcdiag /test:replications

Certain replication events also can be found in the directory service event viewer.

Several types of errors might occur with replication, including errors related to lag or slowness of replication and permission errors. Table 5-1 describes some common problems and their resolution.

TABLE 5-1 Replication problems and solutions

Problem	Resolution
Slow replication	Review event log to determine whether errors occurred. Review site topology. Review intersite replication optimization checklist at *http://technet .microsoft.com/library/cc783025*.
Errors indicating a problem exists with sites and site link information	Ensure that all sites belong to at least one site link and that the site links create an available path to all domain controllers that have a replica of a directory partition. Also, ensure that bridgehead servers are online and that sites have connectivity.
DNS Lookup Failure or RPC server is unavailable	Run dcdiag /test:connectivity to verify DNS CNAME and A records. Restart netlogon (net start netlogon). Verify IP configuration. Verify that zone is dynamic (dcdiag /test:registerindns /dnsdomain:<domain name>). Ping the domain controller, using its GUID-based name.
Access is denied error	Stop the KDC. Purge ticket cache on the local domain controller. Reset the domain controller's account password (netdom /resetpwd). Synchronize the replication partner's domain directory partition with the PDC emulator. Force replication and then restart the KDC (net start KDC).
Access is denied for manual replication	Use repadmin or replmon to force the replication. Verify permissions for replication synchronization.

MORE INFO   **MONITORING AND TROUBLESHOOTING REPLICATION**

See *http://technet.microsoft.com/library/cc755349* for more information on replication monitoring and troubleshooting.

THOUGHT EXPERIMENT
Troubleshooting replication

In this thought experiment, apply what you've learned about this objective. You can find answers the "Answers" section at the end of this chapter.

You now have a replication setup among three sites. You've received reports that replication among those sites isn't working correctly. As part of troubleshooting, you view the event log and notice that you're receiving a DNS error related to replication.

Describe the steps you can take to further troubleshoot this issue.

Objective summary

- Domain controller placement depends largely on the topology necessary for the organization.
- You can divide several roles among multiple servers to enable faster authentication and more reliable directory services for remote sites.
- When considering deploying additional domain controllers or spreading role load among multiple sites, you should take care to ensure that the site links are designed in such a way so as to support replication.
- You can optimize replication traffic by changing the site cost, schedule, and interval.
- Use the repadmin and dcdiag commands to report information about replication and to monitor replication performance.

Objective review

Answer the following questions to test your knowledge of the information in this objective. You can find the answers to these questions and explanations of why each answer choice is correct or incorrect in the "Answers" section at the end of this chapter.

1. When you're designing a replication configuration, which of the following can't be changed?

   A. Site cost

   B. Interval

   C. Traffic shape

   D. Schedule

2. Which of the following is an example of an application that requires a site to be created?

   A. DFSN

   B. GPL

   C. AD DS

   D. FTP

3. Which of the following isn't a server type or role typically considered in topology design?

   A. Global catalog server

   B. Regional domain controller

   C. Operations master role

   D. Site replication server

Objective 5.2: Design a domain controller strategy

When considering a domain controller strategy, you need to look at several factors, including how the various domain controller–related roles should be deployed in an organization as well as the need to divide roles and deploy additional read-only copies of the directory.

This objective covers the following topics:

- Design considerations, including global catalog, operations master roles, Read-Only Domain Controllers (RODCs), partial attribute set, and domain controller cloning

Global catalog and operations master roles

You need to place global catalog servers carefully when your organization has more than one forest. The global catalog contains all objects in the forest, including a full copy of objects in the global catalog's own domain and a read-only copy of objects for all other domains in the forest. A single-forest (and/or multi-domain) scenario should have the global catalog server located on all domain controllers. In a multi-forest scenario, place a global catalog server at the following locations:

- A location that has an application requiring a global catalog server
- A location with more than 100 users
- A site with unreliable connectivity and several roaming users
- A site with reliable connectivity but slow logon performance for roaming users

If none of these criteria are met, you should place a domain controller with universal group membership caching at the location.

Whereas any Active Directory domain controller can write most directory data, certain data can be written only by operations master role servers. Of the several operations master roles, the first three exist at the domain level and are known as *flexible single master operations* (FSMO) roles:

- Primary domain controller (PDC) emulator, which processes password updates
- Relative ID (RID) operations master, which maintains the global RID pool and allocates local RIDs to other domain controllers
- Infrastructure operations master, which maintains a list of security principals from other domains that are members of groups in the local domain

Two other roles exist at the forest level:

- Schema operations master, which controls schema changes
- Domain naming operations master, which controls changes to the directory partitions such as adding and removing domains from the forest

You should place operations master role servers, especially those with PDC and RID responsibilities, in sites with reliable network connectivity. The operations master role is automatically assigned to the first domain controller in a forest. However, these roles can become a resource burden and, as a result, can be assigned to another domain controller.

Only one domain controller serves as the PDC emulator for each domain in the forest, so the PDC emulator role should be placed nearest the largest number of users. The infrastructure master monitors for changes to security principals from other domains added to groups in the local domain. Don't place the infrastructure master on the same server as the global catalog server; otherwise, the infrastructure master won't function. Only on multi-domain forests does the infrastructure server role become important, and then only when multiple servers are sharing the roles.

Read-only domain controllers

Read-only domain controllers (RODCs) have read-only copies of the Active Directory database and the SYSVOL folder. This is helpful for branch office or remote locations that use a local Active Directory Domain Services (AD DS) server but don't require a full, writable copy of AD DS at those locations.

One reason for deploying an RODC is security. RODCs don't replicate changes from remote locations to the main directory, but rather pass changes made to the directory to a writable domain controller. Requests for access to resources outside the RODC-based domain must be passed to a hub site that examines and rewrites the request after verifying access. The hub site does so because the RODC uses a special krbtgt account for accounts whose passwords are cached locally. RODCs have a special Password Replication Policy (PRP) that doesn't allow passwords to be cached by default. Another aspect of RODC security is the Filtered Attribute Set (FAS), which can restrict application data that can be replicated to RODCs.

Another reason for deploying an RODC is manageability. RODCs lend themselves to delegation of administration, enabling local administrators to work with the RODC at their locations. You can accomplish Administrator Role Separation (ARS) with a certain amount of granularity when using RODCs. Further, when applications need to run on a domain controller, an RODC is a good candidate for this type of deployment, assuming that the application doesn't require a writable directory service.

> **NOTE   LOGGING ON**
>
> Logging on to an RODC with a domain administrator account isn't recommended.

In the event of a wide area network (WAN) outage, an RODC can still provide logon capabilities to users at the RODC location. However, several items no longer work when a branch office goes offline, such as password changes and domain joins.

A final reason for deploying an RODC is scalability. RODCs use unidirectional replication, thus lessening the amount of traffic that must pass over a WAN link. Distributed File System (DFS) replication also alleviates some load on the WAN link by using compression and replicating changes only for SYSVOL traffic.

Partial attribute set

As discussed earlier, the global catalog contains a read-only copy of the objects from other
domains in the forest. This partial copy includes only a subset of attributes—those commonly
used for search operations as well as other required attributes. When considered as a whole,
this copy is known as a *partial attribute set* (PAS), which can be changed to help customize the
attributes available for speeding up search operations. When an attribute isn't found in the
local global catalog, the search might be referred to another domain controller.

Domain controller cloning

Virtual domain controllers have been an available deployment option for quite some time.
Windows Server 2012 makes the process of virtual deployment easier by enabling cloning.
Deploying a new virtual domain controller with Windows Server 2012 no longer requires the
use of sysprep.

Active Directory relies heavily on clock-based replication using an increasing number
known as an Update Sequence Number (USN). Each domain controller within an organization
has a unique identity known as an InvocationID. Combining the USN and the InvocationID
creates an identifier that must be unique across the entire forest.

A new identifier called a VM-GenerationID, a feature added in Windows Server 2012, adds
safeguards for virtually deployed domain controllers. The VM-GenerationID is stored in the
msDS-GenerationID attribute in the domain controller's computer object. If a virtual snapshot is used or rolled back, the VM-GenerationID is compared to the original value in the
msDS-GenerationID and, if different, the InvocationID is reset.

Virtualized domain controller cloning is helpful for rapidly deploying test environments or deployment to branch offices. Cloning is also helpful for scaling out when resource capacity of the existing domain controllers are reached.

MORE INFO   **CLONING VIRTUAL DOMAN CONTROLLERS**

See *http://technet.microsoft.com/library/hh831734.aspx* for more information on virtual domain controller cloning.

THOUGHT EXPERIMENT
Deploying roles and servers at a remote site

In this thought experiment, apply what you've learned about this objective. You can find answers the "Answers" section at the end of this chapter.

You're tasked with designing the Active Directory infrastructure for a single site with a remote branch office. This remote branch office has 500 users. You've already deployed much of your Active Directory infrastructure on virtualized domain controllers running at the Windows Server 2012 functional level.

Describe the roles and/or servers that you would deploy at the remote site.

Objective summary

- Global catalog servers and operations master roles are important in an Active Directory infrastructure. Several recommendations have been made for their use and placement.

- Read-only domain controllers (RODCs) provide a read-only copy of the directory database and SYSVOL. They are helpful for branch locations that warrant an Active Directory server or for applications that need to be installed on a domain controller.

- The partial attribute set in the global catalog stores certain attributes from all domains within the forest.

- Windows Server 2012 makes virtual domain controller cloning much easier by alleviating the sysprep requirements.

Objective review

Answer the following questions to test your knowledge of the information in this objective. You can find the answers to these questions and explanations of why each answer choice is correct or incorrect in the "Answers" section at the end of this chapter.

1. Which role processes password updates?

   A. Global catalog

   B. Branch Office

   C. PDC Emulator

   D. Partial Attribute Set

2. Which attribute was created to track the virtual machine in a domain controller scenario?

   A. VM-GenerationID

   B. InvocationID

   C. RID

   D. Global Identifier

3. At least how many users should a location have to require a global catalog server?

   A. 500

   B. 250

   C. 1,000

   D. 100

Objective 5.3: Design and implement a branch office infrastructure

Branch offices refer to remote locations or even locations managed distinctly from the organization's main data center and management operations. Branch offices frequently have specific requirements to help them operate smoothly. Therefore, designing a branch office infrastructure is an important task.

This objective covers the following topics:

- Design considerations, including RODC, Universal Group Membership Caching (UGMC), global catalog, Domain Name System (DNS), Dynamic Host Configuration Protocol (DHCP), and BranchCache
- Implementing confidential attributes
- Delegating administration

- Modifying the filtered attribute set
- Configuring Password Replication Policy
- Configuring Hash Publication

Understanding branch office infrastructure design considerations

During the design of a branch office infrastructure, your overall goal is to provide reliability for remote locations, regardless of the connectivity status back at the main data center. At the same time, you need to keep the management overhead of additional infrastructure to a minimum.

RODC, global catalog, and UGMC

RODCs are a primary means with which branch offices can achieve the goals of local service and data availability, without the burden of extra administrative overhead. Objective 5.2, "Design a domain controller strategy," discussed several design considerations for both RODC and the global catalog.

In a multi-domain forest scenario, Universal Group Membership Caching (UGMC) prevents additional traffic from crossing the WAN for initial user logon. UGMC is deployed for branch offices in multi-domain forests that don't have a local global catalog server at the branch office. If a global catalog server is to be deployed, UGMC isn't necessary.

> **MORE INFO**   **GLOBAL CATALOG ARCHITECTURE AND OPERATIONS**
>
> For more information on the architecture and operations of the global catalog, including UGMC, see *http://technet.microsoft.com/library/cc775731*.

DNS and DHCP

Domain Name System (DNS) servers should be placed with a domain controller, even an RODC. So when you deploy a domain controller for a branch office, you should also deploy the DNS service on that domain controller. The benefit of doing so means that the branch office can continue with DNS lookups, even if the link to the data center is unavailable.

For an RODC deployment, you should use primary read-only zone types. The RODC then copies all the application directory partitions, including the domain partition, ForestDNSZones, and DomainDNSZones. If the domain controller at the branch office isn't an RODC, you can operate the DNS server in caching mode or as a secondary to the main DNS server, with the latter option being more complicated to initially configure.

You can also operate Dynamic Host Configuration Protocol (DHCP) on the same server with Active Directory, although the decision to do so rests largely with the amount of traffic and resource usage already on that domain controller, as well as the amount of administrative overhead incurred by implementing an additional server to handle DHCP traffic at a branch office. Three deployment options are available for DHCP at a branch office:

- Deployment with Active Directory and DNS
- Deployment with File and Print services
- Deployment with a networking server, such as Internet Security and Acceleration (ISA)

The decision to deploy a DHCP server rests on the need for availability at that location, along with the reliability and overhead for the WAN link between the branch office and the data center—essentially, the same set of decisions that go into deployment of any services for the branch office.

> **MORE INFO** **DESIGNING A BRANCH OFFICE**
>
> See the Branch Office Infrastructure Solution at *http://www.microsoft.com/en-us/ download/details.aspx?id=22199* for additional information on design of a branch office.

BranchCache

BranchCache helps reduce network traffic over WAN links by locally caching content accessed from the data center or cloud-based content. BranchCache operates in two modes: *distributed cache mode* disperses cached content among client computers, and *hosted cache mode* stores the cached content on a server at the branch office. The choice of cache mode becomes a central decision when designing a deployment with BranchCache.

> **EXAM TIP**
>
> You should be familiar with the difference between hosted and distributed modes for the exam, including when to use each.

Hosted cache mode has the benefit of increased cache availability because the content cache doesn't rely on whether a given client is online. With hosted cache mode, content also can be shared on multi-subnet branch offices, a scenario that isn't possible with distributed cache mode. However, hosted cache mode requires deployment of a server for hosting the cache and therefore incurs additional administrative overhead.

The BranchCache feature needs to be installed on select web and application servers for content to be cached.

Follow these guidelines for determining which mode is appropriate for BranchCache in a given situation. Use distributed cache mode when

- The branch office has fewer than 100 users and has no other servers deployed in the branch.
- The branch office has multiple subnets, each with fewer than 100 users per subnet.

Use hosted cache mode when

- The branch office has more than 100 users, either in a single subnet or multiple subnets.
- The branch office has other servers deployed on which BranchCache can be installed.

> **MORE INFO** **BRANCHCACHE**
>
> See *http://technet.microsoft.com/library/hh831696* for more information on BranchCache and *http://technet.microsoft.com/library/ee731918* for the BranchCache Design Guide.

Implementing confidential attributes

You can mark certain attributes as confidential within a domain. The typical reason for doing so is to prevent unauthorized individuals from seeing the data marked as confidential. To mark an attribute as confidential, you use ADSI Edit and typically the ldifde tool.

> **NOTE** **CONFIDENTIAL ATTRIBUTES**
>
> Confidential attributes apply to all domain controllers, including RODCs.

Although you can use ADSI Edit to mark an attribute as confidential, the scenario described here illustrates the use of ldifde, which is typically used for bulk or scripted operations. To mark an attribute as confidential, first view the attribute in ADSI Edit. For example, Figure 5-1 shows the documentLocation object found at CN=documentLocation,CN=Schema,CN=Configuration. Notice that the value for SearchFlags is 0x0, meaning that no flags are set for this attribute.

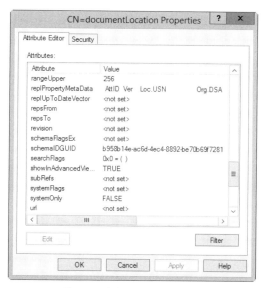

FIGURE 5-1 The searchFlags attribute is set to 0x0.

Open a command prompt as Administrator and run the following command, again using documentLocation as the example and the adventure-works.com domain:

```
ldifde -d "CN=documentLocation,CN=Schema,CN=Configuration,DC=adventure-works,DC=com" -f
en_ldif -l searchflags
```

The ldifde command runs and produces a file in the current directory called en_ldif. The contents of that file look like the following:

```
dn: CN=documentLocation,CN=Schema,CN=Configuration,DC=adventure-works,DC=com
changetype: add
searchFlags: 0
```

Edit the file with a text editor such as Notepad. Set the changetype to modify, add the line replace: searchFlags, change the searchFlags value to 128, and add a - at the end. The final result looks like this:

```
dn: CN=documentLocation,CN=Schema,CN=Configuration,DC=adventure-works,DC=com
changetype: modify
replace: searchFlags
searchFlags: 128
-
```

Save that file as en-confidential.

Now import the file with the following command:

```
ldifde -i -f en-confidential
```

After this command completes, examine the searchFlag value through ADSI Edit again. Notice, as shown in Figure 5-2, that the value is now 0x80 (bitwise representation of 128), reflecting the change that you made.

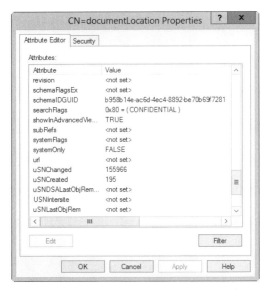

FIGURE 5-2 Marking documentLocation as Confidential, as seen through ADSI Edit.

Delegating administration

Administration of an RODC can be delegated at the time of installation through a feature called Administrator Role Separation (ARS). Delegation can be done to a user or group. This user has local administrative rights (not Domain Admin rights) to perform administration tasks on the RODC.

RODC delegation can be configured when the domain controller is being configured. Alternatively, delegating administration after installation is accomplished through Active Directory Users and Computers on the Managed By tab of the RODC's Properties sheet, as shown in Figure 5-3.

FIGURE 5-3 The Managed By tab is used to delegate administration of an RODC.

MORE INFO **RODC ADMINISTRATION**

See *http://technet.microsoft.com/library/cc755310* for more information on RODC administration, including delegation of administration.

Modifying the filtered attribute set

The Filtered Attribute Set (FAS) is the set of attributes not replicated to an RODC. The default FAS contains the following:

- ms-PKI-DPAPIMasterKeys
- ms-PKI-AccountCredentials
- ms-PKI-RoamingTimeStamp
- ms-FVE-KeyPackage
- ms-FVE-RecoveryPassword
- ms-TPM-OwnerInformation

Items you place in the FAS aren't replicated, in case the RODC is placed at a lower security site and then compromised. Therefore, you can add items to the FAS so that they aren't replicated.

> **MORE INFO   FAS CONCEPTS**
>
> See *http://technet.microsoft.com/library/cc753459%28WS.10%29.aspx* for more information on the concepts surrounding the FAS.

Like confidential attributes, the FAS is modified using the ldifde tool. For example, to mark an attribute as being part of the FAS, first view the attribute in ADSI Edit. Figure 5-4 shows the secretary object found at CN=secretary,CN=Schema,CN=Configuration. Notice that the value for SearchFlags is 0x0, meaning that no flags are set for this attribute.

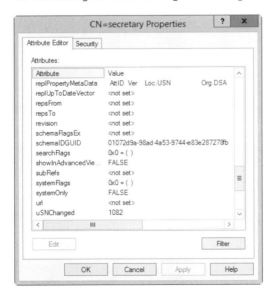

FIGURE 5-4 Viewing the searchFlags to determine if any are now set for this object.

Open a command prompt as Administrator and run the following command, again using secretary as the example and the adventure-works.com domain:

```
ldifde -d "CN=secretary,CN=Schema,CN=Configuration,DC=adventure-works,DC=com" -f en_ldif
-l searchflags
```

The ldifde command produces a file in the current directory called en_ldif. The contents of that file look like the following:

```
dn: CN=secretary,CN=Schema,CN=Configuration,DC=adventure-works,DC=com
changetype: add
searchFlags: 0
```

Edit the file with a text editor such as Notepad. Set the changetype to modify, add the line replace: searchFlags, change the searchFlags value to 512, and add a - at the end. The final result looks like this:

```
dn: CN=secretary,CN=Schema,CN=Configuration,DC=adventure-works,DC=com
changetype: modify
replace: searchFlags
searchFlags: 512
-
```

Save that file as en-confidential.

Now import the file with the following command:

```
ldifde -i -f en-confidential
```

Examine the searchFlag value through ADSI Edit again. Notice in Figure 5-5 that the value is now 0x200 (bitwise representation of 512), reflecting the change that you made.

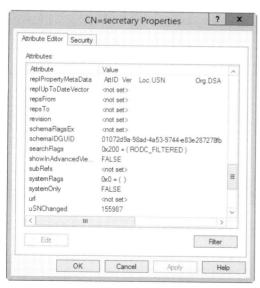

FIGURE 5-5 The object's searchFlags is now set to 0x200 = (RODC_FILTERED), which indicates that it's part of the FAS.

MORE INFO   **FAS ATTRIBUTES**

See *http://technet.microsoft.com/en-us/library/cc754794%28v=ws.10%29* for more information on setting attributes for the FAS.

Configuring Password Replication Policy

The Password Replication Policy can be configured when the AD DS role is being configured or afterward through Active Directory Users and Computers, within the Password Replication Policy tab of the RODC's Properties sheet, shown in Figure 5-6.

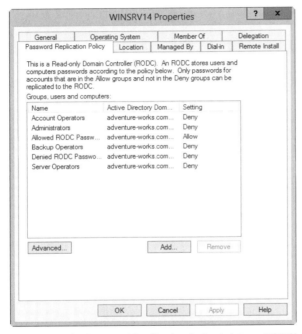

FIGURE 5-6 The Password Replication Policy tab in an RODC's Properties sheet.

You can add accounts to be cached by clicking Add. You can allow the accounts to have their credentials cached by clicking Allow Passwords For The Account To Replicate To This RODC or deny by clicking Deny Passwords For The Account From Replicating To This RODC, as shown in Figure 5-7.

FIGURE 5-7 Adding a security principal to the Password Replication Policy.

Clicking Advanced in the Properties sheet brings up the Advanced Password Replication Policy dialog box, as shown in Figure 5-8.

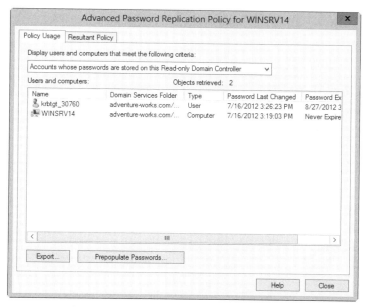

FIGURE 5-8 Advanced properties for Password Replication Policy.

The accounts shown in Figure 5-8 are stored on the RODC. You can clear this list with the following command, run as a Domain Admin:

```
repadmin /prp delete <server> auth2 /all
```

The Resultant Policy tab shows whether an account is allowed to cache its password at the RODC.

A best practice related to RODCs is to create a separate group for each RODC, grant each group the right to cache passwords only on that RODC, and then prepopulate the RODC with the appropriate accounts.

Configuring Hash Publication

You configure Hash Publication in the Group Policy Object Editor, within the Computer Configuration | Administrative Templates | Network | Lanman Server hierarchy.

Double-clicking Hash Publication For BranchCache in the details pane opens the Hash Publication for BranchCache dialog box, as shown in Figure 5-9.

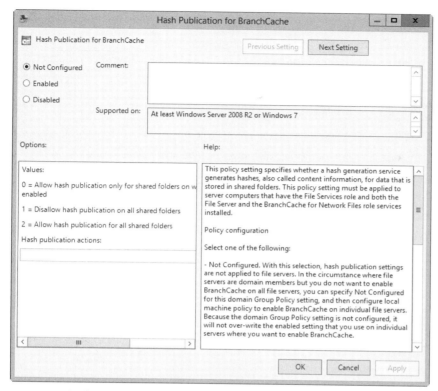

FIGURE 5-9 Configuring Hash Publication For BranchCache.

Select Enabled to choose one of three settings:

- 0 = Allow hash publication only for shared folders on which BranchCache is enabled
- 1 = Disallow hash publication for all shared folders
- 2 = Allow hash publication for all shared folders

THOUGHT EXPERIMENT
Deploying a branch office

In this thought experiment, apply what you've learned about this objective. You can find answers the "Answers" section at the end of this chapter.

You'll be deploying a branch office. This branch office will have about 200 users. The branch office currently has no servers at its location. The WAN link will be two T-1s.

Describe the authentication, DNS, DHCP, and related items that you might configure for this scenario.

Objective summary

- Read-only domain controllers (RODCs) and global catalog servers are an important part of a branch office design because they can increase availability while reducing WAN traffic.
- UGMC is deployed for branch offices in multi-domain forests that don't have a local global catalog server at the branch office.
- You should deploy a DNS server at a branch office to ensure availability of the service.
- BranchCache operates in two modes: distributed cache and hosted cache.
- Distributed cache mode disperses the content among client computers in the branch office, whereas hosted cache mode stores the content on a server in the branch office.
- To create confidential attributes, modify the searchFlags attribute to a value of 128.
- You can handle administration of RODCs when the AD DS role is being configured or afterward on the Managed By tab of the server's Properties sheet.
- You can add an object to the Filtered Attribute Set by setting searchFlags to 512.
- You configure Password Replication Policy through Active Directory Users and Computers, and you can configure the accounts that are allowed to be cached on the RODC.
- Hash Publication is configured through Group Policy Object Editor.

Objective review

Answer the following questions to test your knowledge of the information in this objective. You can find the answers to these questions and explanations of why each answer choice is correct or incorrect in the "Answers" section at the end of this chapter.

1. Distributed cache mode is appropriate for all the following except (choose all that apply):

   A. A multi-subnet branch office with 75 users per subnet

   B. A single subnet branch office with 200 users

   C. A branch office with 80 users

   D. A branch office with 51 users

2. When a primary read-only zone is deployed with an RODC at a branch office, which of the following zones or data types is not copied?

   A. ForestDNSZones

   B. DomainDNSZones

   C. Domain Partition

   D. Root Primary Zone

3. Which of the following isn't included in the default FAS?

   A. ms-FVE-KeyPackage

   B. ms-AD-Password-FV

   C. ms-FVE-RecoveryPassword

   D. ms-TPM-OwnerInformation

4. To be marked as part of the FAS, searchFlags should be set to which value?

   A. 0

   B. 64

   C. 128

   D. 512

Chapter summary

- When designing placement of domain controllers you will need to examine the topology necessary for the organization.
- You can divide roles between servers to better service remote sites and provide faster authentication and more reliability.
- Replication traffic can be optimized by changing site cost, schedule, and interval.
- Read-only domain controllers (RODCs) provide read-only directories and are helpful for branch locations.
- Using a DNS server at a branch office to ensure availability of the service is good practice.

Answers

This section contains the solutions to the thought experiments and answers to the objective review questions in this chapter.

Objective 5.1: Thought experiment

Troubleshooting DNS-related issues is sometimes difficult and is certainly somewhat more art than science. The repadmin /showrepl command might show additional information and could be run as part of troubleshooting. The output from that command would confirm the GUID of the server so that you could ping the server based on its GUID. You also should ensure that the netlogon service is started, although it's likely that other problems would occur if that service wasn't running.

Verifying connectivity to the server(s) reporting the replication problem can be the first step as well. From there, using nslookup to verify the configuration of basic CNAME and A records for the server(s) in question would be helpful too. The dcdiag /test:connectivity command is helpful, as is dcdiag /test:registerindns /dnsdomain:<domain name> and other dcdiag tests related to DNS.

Objective 5.1: Review

1. **Correct answer:** C

   A. **Incorrect:** Site cost can be changed.

   B. **Incorrect:** Interval can be changed.

   C. **Correct:** Traffic Shape isn't a factor that can be altered.

   D. **Incorrect:** The schedule for replication can be changed.

2. **Correct answer:** A

   A. **Correct:** Distributed File System Namespaces (DFSN) was identified as an application that would require a site to be created.

   B. **Incorrect:** GPL isn't a real application.

   C. **Incorrect:** AD DS was not identified as an application that would require its own site.

   D. **Incorrect:** FTP was not identified as an application that would require its own site.

3. **Correct answer:** D

  A. **Incorrect:** The location of the global catalog server is considered for topology design

  B. **Incorrect:** The location of regional domain controllers is considered for topology design.

  C. **Incorrect:** The operations master role is considered for topology design.

  D. **Correct:** Site Replication Server isn't a real role and therefore not considered for topology design.

Objective 5.2: Thought experiment

In all likelihood, you would place a global catalog server at the remote location because you have more than 100 users. However, you might be tempted to place an RODC at the remote location also. The difficulty is that the problem statement didn't indicate whether the remote site had administrators or how reliable the connectivity is. If connectivity is reliable, an operations master role would also be a viable option to place at the remote location.

Objective 5.2: Review

1. **Correct answer:** C

  A. **Incorrect:** Global catalog isn't responsible for password updates.

  B. **Incorrect:** Branch Office isn't a component of Active Directory

  C. **Correct:** The PDC Emulator processes password updates.

  D. **Incorrect:** Partial Attribute Set isn't related to password updates.

2. **Correct answer:** A

  A. **Correct:** The VM-GenerationID is a new attribute used to track the ID of the domain controller.

  B. **Incorrect:** The InvocationID is an existing attribute that exists both for virtualized and non-virtualized environments.

  C. **Incorrect:** The RID isn't a new attribute.

  D. **Incorrect:** The Global Identifier isn't related to domain controllers.

3. **Correct answer:** D

  A. **Incorrect:** 500 isn't the recommendation.

  B. **Incorrect:** 250 isn't the recommendation.

  C. **Incorrect:** 1,000 isn't the recommendation.

  D. **Correct:** 100 users is the recommended amount after which you should deploy a global catalog server.

Objective 5.3: Thought experiment

You would likely add an RODC for this location to ensure that authentication traffic doesn't pass through the WAN, which might be lower speed than necessary. A DNS server should be deployed on the same server as the RODC, and the DHCP service can likely run off of this server as well. Nothing was noted for the location of content or files for this location, so you do not have enough information to determine whether BranchCache would be warranted. You have more than 100 users, so it's likely that a global catalog server also would be deployed. This would alleviate the need for UGMC.

Objective 5.3: Review

1. **Correct answer:** B

   A. **Incorrect:** A multi-subnet branch office with 75 users per subnet can use distributed cache mode.

   B. **Correct:** A single subnet branch office with 200 users exceeds the 100-user recommendation for distributed cache mode.

   C. **Incorrect:** A branch office with 80 users is below the 100-user recommendation.

   D. **Incorrect:** A branch office with 51 users is below the 100-user recommendation.

2. **Correct answer:** D

   A. **Incorrect:** ForestDNSZones is copied in this scenario.

   B. **Incorrect:** DomainDNSZones is copied in this scenario.

   C. **Incorrect:** Domain Partition is copied in this scenario.

   D. **Correct:** Root Primary Zone isn't a real zone, but sounds like it could be.

3. **Correct answer:** B

   A. **Incorrect:** ms-FVE-KeyPackage is included in the default FAS.

   B. **Correct:** ms-AD-Password-FV isn't included in the default FAS.

   C. **Incorrect:** ms-FVE-RecoveryPassword is included in the default FAS.

   D. **Incorrect:** ms-TPM-OwnerInformation is included in the default FAS.

4. **Correct answer:** D

   A. **Incorrect:** 0 isn't the correct answer.

   B. **Incorrect:** 64 isn't the correct answer.

   C. **Incorrect:** 128 is used to mark an object as confidential, not mark it as part of the FAS.

   D. **Correct:** 512 is the correct value to mark an object as part of the FAS.

Index

Symbols

A

H

I

U

V

About the Author

STEVE SUEHRING is a technology architect providing both vision and implementation assistance to organizations of all sizes. Steve specializes in large-scale, big-picture uses of technology to solve business problems with a focus on how to meet an organization's goals. His experience enables him to have a unique perspective on interoperability among the technologies available in today's enterprises. Steve has spoken at events around the world, served as an editor for a technology magazine, and authored several books on a wide range of subjects including programming, security, and enterprise administration. You can follow him at his web site *http://www.braingia.org* and *@stevesuehring* on Twitter.

What do you think of this book?

We want to hear from you!

To participate in a brief online survey, please visit:

microsoft.com/learning/booksurvey

Tell us how well this book meets your needs—what works effectively, and what we can do better. Your feedback will help us continually improve our books and learning resources for you.

Thank you in advance for your input!